CW00502751

DIECAST   RAILWAYS   TOY FIGURES   TINPLATE

» Publisher
Claire Ingram
claire.ingram@warnersgroup.co.uk

» Editor
Cathy Herron
cathyh@warnersgroup.co.uk

» Advertising Manager
Kristina Green 01778 392096
kristina.green@warnersgroup.co.uk

» Head of Design
Lynn Wright
lynnw@warnersgroup.co.uk

» Production Manager
Nicola Lock 01778 392420
nicola.lock@warnersgroup.co.uk

» Production Assistant
Charlotte Bamford 01778 395081
charlotte.bamford@warnersgroup.co.uk

» Marketing Manager
Katherine Brown 01778 395502
katherine.brown@warnersgroup.co.uk

» Marketing Executive
Luke Hider 01778 395085
luke.hider@warnersgroup.co.uk

Toy Collectors Price Guide 2022 is published annually by Warners Group Publications Plc, The Maltings, West Street, Bourne, Lincolnshire PE10 9PH, UK.

» Newstrade Distribution
This magazine is distributed by:
Warners Group Publications Ltd
Tel: 01778 391150

This publication is printed by Warners
01778 395111

Welcome

I t gives me great pleasure to welcome you to our latest annual *Toy Collectors Price Guide*, which gives you an estimate on how much your vintage toy collection might be worth. We've scoured auction house results from around the country to bring you a super selection of collectables, along with detailed descriptions and large, colour photographs.

Whether you collect diecast vehicles, model locomotives, toy figures, TV and film memorabilia, tinplate or something a little more unusual, I'm sure you'll find plenty to tickle your fancy in this year's guide. In the pages ahead you'll find over 1000 listings, worth more than £400,000 in total.

We all hope you enjoy this year's edition and that 2022 continues to be a bumper year for toy collecting. Happy collecting everyone!

Cathy Herron
Editor

Cathy

CONTENTS

Warners Group Publications is the UK's leading publisher of collecting titles including *Collectors Gazette, Diecast Collector, British Railway Modelling* and *Ramsay's British Diecast Model Toys Catalogue.*

We have compiled this guide using information supplied directly from auction houses the world over – some prices realised are listed as hammer prices while others include commissions. More information about specific items can be obtained from each auctioneer direct. Other useful collecting information can be found on **www.collectors-club-of-great-britain.co.uk**

Toy Collectors Price Guide, Warners Group Publications, West Street, Bourne, Lincs PE10 9PH. Tel: **01778 391167**

Guide to...
Buying toys online

Life is a bit different for all of us these days. We might be staying at home a bit more, or being more careful where we venture out to. While that means we have the opportunity to sort through collections, find models that have long been forgotten and catch up on all those back issues of your favourite collecting magazine, it also means that regular swapmeets and auctions might be a bit thin on the ground.

But not quite! More auction houses have started to run toy sales through their own websites or via online platforms such as The Saleroom. You can still get your toy fix, but now from the comfort of your sofa.

Here we will try to de-mystify all things 'digital' for you:

ONLINE AUCTIONS

All websites are slightly different, however the process of bidding online is generally the same. If you are in any doubt, staff at the auction houses will be at the end of the phone and will be happy to help you.

1 BROWSE

Find the object you want to buy by searching for it. You can browse by category or by looking through the auctioneers' online catalogues.

You can contact the auction house to ask questions about the item you are interested in. One key thing to remember is that at an auction it is up to you as the bidder to satisfy yourself about the condition of an item before you bid. Make sure that you read the lot description and check the photos!

2 REGISTER

Once you have found the item you want to bid on, you will need to register

Image courtesy of Wallis and Wallis.

with the auction house that it is selling it. This means that you will need to create a secure account but the website will walk you through the process step by step. You may also need to register your credit/debit card so that payment can be made.

3 BID

A convenient option might be to place a maximum bid before the auction starts. This is the highest amount you are willing to pay for a lot. Then sit back and relax.

Once the auction starts, sites such as thesaleroom.com will place your bids for you, only ever bidding just enough to do keep you in the lead and it will never go beyond your limit. If nobody else bids more than your maximum bid then you will win the lot.

Alternatively, you can bid live during the auction. You can do this on your PC, tablet or mobile phone. You'll be joining the thrill of the event and competing against other buyers in real time. You will be able to see and hear the auction as it progresses and place your bids as the items you want to buy come up.

4 PAY AND TAKE IT AWAY OR GET IT DELIVERED

If you are the successful bidder, then the item is yours, congratulations! The auction house will usually contact you to arrange payment once the auction has ended or you can contact them. Some will provide a way to pay online, others will take payment by card or bank transfer.

Some auction houses will offer a packing and delivery service, others will arrange to keep your item in storage until the government advice allows for it to be collected. Most auction houses will recommend local or national courier companies that will pack, pick up and deliver your item to you. There will be a charge for any packing and delivery service that you use.

TOP TIPS

• **Check the details** - Make sure you don't get too swept away with the excitement of the find, and make a bid before reading all of the product information carefully. Take your time, and make sure you've noted the condition.

• **Set your maximum bid** - The last few minutes of an auction can be really exciting, but make sure you don't go above what you intended to pay – or out-bid yourself. You can utilise the auction house's maximum bid tool so this doesn't happen. Also bear in mind additional auction fees and provisions and factor these into the final price.

• **Start low** - The starting price of an item is set by the initial valuation of the auction house, and provides a good indicator of what your opening bid should be. It's advisable to start low as this gets the bidding off to a good start, but bear in mind that the actual hammer price can be considerably higher than the starting price.

MONTHLY NEWSPAPER FOR TOY COLLECTORS

>> GERRY ANDERSON COLLECTABLES
REMEMBERING MODELS FROM THE THUNDERBIRDS

COLLECTORS GAZETTE

September 2021 • Issue No 450 • www.ccofgb.co.uk • £3.99

Tempting TINPLATE

Put a price on your toy treasures, with our latest auction price guide!

+ EVENT REPORT
Visiting Malvern as swapmeets restart

PLUS
The latest hobby news inside!

>> INSURE YOUR COLLECTION
Hints and tips on how to protect your models should disaster strike

>> FAMOUS FAC[ES]
THE AVENGERS
Looking at the models made popular by the Sixties TV programme

>> VALUE YOUR MODEL COL[LECTION]
8-PAGES OF THE LATEST TOY SALE R[ESULTS]

COLLECTORS GAZETTE

October 2021 • Issue No 451 • www.ccofgb.co.uk • £3.99

FUN WITH Figures

>> 10-MINUTE TOY EXPERT
All there is to know about collecting vintage Meccano

>> PLONK & [...] WITH HORN[BY]
Why every rail[way] collection shou[ld have a] model village o[...]

[...]E YOUR MODEL COLLECTION!
[...]S OF THE LATEST TOY SALE RESULTS INSIDE

[CO]LLECTORS GAZETTE

[...]ELLING IN

Worlds only newspaper dedicated to toy collecting

INSIDE EVERY ISSUE:

→ Latest auction, toyfairs and event news.
→ Features on traditional and nostalgic toys and models.

→ Price guides.
→ The very latest releases can be found from all the major manufacturers in the industry.

To see our latest subscription offers visit: ccofgb.uk/gaz-tcpg22 or call 01778 392480 quoting GAZ/TCPG22

READ THE MAGAZINE ANYWHERE!
Did you know... *Collectors Gazette* is also available as a digital edition! Download issues directly to your devices and read wherever you are.
Visit pktmags.com/gaz-tcpg22 to find out more.

Introduction to...
Collecting
Diecast

A rguably one of the most popular area of collecting is the diecast market. Whether you enjoy picking up replicas of iconic road cars, vintage sportscars or even circus vehicles, then diecast collecting is certainly the thing for you.

Although originally made as hardwearing toys that were meant to be bashed around by enthusiastic children during playtime, diecast vehicles have now become extremely sought after collectables, with people happy to pay big money to acquire some of the more unusual pieces or those still in their original boxes.

The big names within the world of diecast (at least in the UK) are undoubtedly Corgi and Dinky - two arch rivals who dominated the 1960s, a period which is often

considered to be the golden era of diecast production. As such the market for Dinky or Corgi models from this period remains bouyant and we've seen some consistently high prices for particularly scarce or top quality diecast replicas.

Of course, they're not the only manufacturers and there are numerous others that regularly sell well at auction - just take your pick from the likes of Spot-On, Benbros, Matchbox, Hot Wheels and more.

In the case of Matchbox, the description is key because the company often produced subtle variations of the same model. For example you might have a Matchbox 25a 56 Bedford 12cwt Van, which is reguarly quoted as being worth £40-50 and then wonder why another Bedford 12cwt makes around £3,000! Well, in the case of Matchbox, it's

all in the wheels. Your common-or-garden variety Bedford has grey wheels, whereas that top end variation has the much rarer black plastic wheels. So, a good tip when you're looking through the following pages is to take great notice of the detailed auctioneer descriptions because a slight change in the wheel colour could make the difference between £10 and £1,000!

Of course, as with most collectables, condition is everything for diecast models. The fact that they were designed as play-things means that some will have chipped paint, scuffs or even parts missing. As a result, serious buyers are happy to pay top whack for those models still in good condition. But it's not just the replica that has to be mint because the box is now equally important as the model itself. Again, look at the

descriptions from auctioneers because they pay great attention to the quality of the box - are there any tears, is a flap missing, is the cellophane window damaged? All of these problems will affect the final valuation.

That's not to say that only mint in box diecast models make the big money at auction though because there are some particularly early pieces from before World War II that are sought after no matter what their condition is. So, if you think you've stumbled across an older piece, do your homework to find out how old it is... or just take it along to one of the numerous valuation days at auction houses up and down the country because their experts will be quick to tell you if you're sitting on a goldmine or whether you've got a bit of an old banger! ∎

Matchbox Super Kings K132 Iveco Turntable Fire Engine, pre-production trial model (model released as Magirus Deutz) - bare metal cab with roof-light cut-outs, red plastic rear body, bare metal turntable with silver-grey plastic ladder, bare metal chassis with Matchbox International England K131-2-8 base text & 1986 copyright date. Excellent plus. Sold for £520, Vectis, October.

Matchbox Regular Wheels No 6b Euclid Quarry Truck, unlisted Stannard Code with very rare factory wheel error - with cab door decals, type C cab windows, type B tipper base with cross brace. Excellent in excellent plus scarce late issue type D2 box. Sold for £420, Vectis, October.

Matchbox King Size G8 Gift Set, K1 Foden Hoveringham Tipper Truck; K11 Fordson Super Major Tractor & Far Tipping Trailer with orange plastic hubs; K12 Foden BP Heavy Wreck Truck ; K15 Merryweather Turntable Fire Engine with Kent Fire Brigade decals. Near mint to mint in good plus type E window box with fair inner vac-form tray. Sold for £160, Vectis, October.

Matchbox King Size K15 Merryweather Turntable Fire Engine, turquoise green windows, Kent Fire Brigade & shield decals, gloss black base, without tow guide. Near mint in near mint type E2 box complete with inner card packing tray. Sold for £60, Vectis, October.

Matchbox Superfast No 13c Snorkel Fire Engine, Brazilian issue - bright red body, dark yellow hoist & platform, dark blue windows, bare metal base, 5-arch wheels. Excellent in fair to good Brazilian box. Sold for £120, Vectis, October.

Matchbox Superfast No 29a American La France Fire Pumper Truck, red with white plastic rear deck and ladder accessories. Mint in excellent type F3 transitional box. Sold for £100, Vectis, October.

Matchbox Superfast No 35a Merryweather Marquis Fire Engine, promotional issue "Flame Proof Wool" - bright red body, 5-spoke wide wheels with black twin rivet axle clips. Excellent plus in good to good plus box. Sold for £1600, Vectis, October.

Matchbox Superfast No 57a Land Rover Fire Truck, red body (darker shade) with silver trim to front bumper, cut-out Kent Fire Brigade & shield door labels, grey plastic base, 5-spoke narrow wheels with black axle clips. Mint in excellent plus "New" type G box. Sold for £130, Vectis, October.

Matchbox Superfast 1975 US Issue Emergency Rescue Gift Set, No 16a Badger Radar Truck; 20b Range Rover Police Patrol; 22c Blaze Buster Fire Engine; 46b Stretcha Fetcha Ambulance; 64c Fire Chief Car; 74b Toe Joe. Near mint to mint in good plus window box. Sold for £90, Vectis, October.

Matchbox Superfast G-12 Rescue Gift Set, No 16a Badger Radar Truck; 20b Range Rover Police Patrol; 22c Blaze Buster Fire Engine; 46b Stretcha Fetcha Ambulance; 64c Fire Chief Car; 74b Toe Joe. Near mint to mint in excellent window box. Sold for £110, Vectis, October.

Dinky pre-war (Type 1) No 28a Delivery Van "Hornby Trains, British & Guaranteed", yellow body - extremely rare, one of the hardest of the 28 Series Vans to find. Fair condition. Sold for £1200, Vectis, October.

Matchbox Superfast No 34c Chevy Pro Stocker empty box, for a pre-production colour trial model, showing correct illustration of white body with green tampo and racing number 88 (model never released in these colours). Good plus with light creasing. Sold for £1000, Vectis, October.

Dinky Toys No 401 Coventry Climax Forklift Truck, burnt orange, black mast and steering wheel, green forks and ridged hubs with grey treaded tyres, light tan driver figure. Good plus to excellent in good plus blue and yellow lift off lid box with correct inner packing pieces. Sold for £40, Vectis, October.

Dinky Toys No 430 Commer Breakdown Lorry "Dinky Service", red cab and chassis, grey back and jib, silver trim, blue plastic hubs with black treaded tyres, with windows. Excellent in good blue and yellow lift off lid box. Sold for £420, Vectis, October.

Dinky Toys No 511 Guy (1st Type) 4-ton Lorry, red cab, chassis and ridged hubs with black smooth tyres, fawn back, tow hook, silver trim. Excellent in good plus green lift off lid box with "Hudson Dobson" label to side. Sold for £220, Vectis, October.

Dinky Toys No 514 Guy (1st Type) "Slumberland" Van, red including ridged hubs with black smooth tyres, silver trim. Good plus in good blue lift off lid box with paper label. Sold for £90, Vectis, October.

Dinky Toys No 531 Leyland Comet Lorry, red cab and chassis, yellow stake back and ridged hubs with grey treaded tyres, silver trim, metal tow hook. Good plus in good plus blue lift off lid box with paper label. Sold for £50, Vectis, October.

Dinky Toys No 532 Leyland Comet Wagon, hinged tailboard, two-tone blue, light beige Supertoy hubs with grey treaded tyres. Excellent in good blue lift off lid box with paper label. Sold for £60, Vectis, October.

Dinky Toys No 581 Horse Box "British Railways Express Horse Box Hire Service", maroon including Supertoy hubs with grey treaded tyres, silver trim. Good plus in good box with paper label. Sold for £140, Vectis, October.

Dinky Toys No 581 EXPORT ISSUE Horse Box "Express Horse Van Hire Service", maroon body, silver trim, red Supertoy hubs with black treaded tyres. Good plus to excellent in good box with correct "Hudson Dobson" label to side, with correct inner packing pieces. Sold for £180, Vectis, October.

Dinky Toys No 901 Foden (2nd Type) Diesel 8-wheeled Wagon, red cab, chassis and Supertoy hubs with black treaded tyres, fawn back, silver trim, metal tow hook. Excellent in good box. Sold for £70, Vectis, October.

Dinky Toys No 905 Foden (2nd Type) Flat Truck with chains, red cab and chassis, Supertoy hubs with black treaded tyres, grey back, silver trim, metal tow hook. Excellent plus in good plus blue and white striped lift off lid box. Sold for £100, Vectis, October.

Dinky Toys No 917 Guy (1st Type) "Spratt's" Delivery Van, two-tone cream, red including Supertoy hubs with black smooth tyres, silver trim. Excellent plus in good box. Sold for £160, Vectis, October.

Dinky Toys No 919 Guy (2nd Type) "Robertson's Golden Shred" Van, red, silver trim, yellow Supertoy hubs with black smooth tyres. Good plus in good plus box with yellow "Hudson Dobson" label to side. Sold for £360, Vectis, October.

Dinky Toys No 923 Big Bedford "Heinz 57 Varieties" Van, red cab and chassis, yellow back and Supertoy hubs with grey treaded tyres, silver trim. Good plus to excellent in good plus box. Sold for £90, Vectis, October.

Dinky Toys No 930 Bedford Pallet Jekta "Dinky Toys" Delivery Van, two-tone yellow, Supertoy hubs with black treaded tyres, with 3 yellow plastic pallets, silver trim. Good plus in good plus box, with inner packing piece and ring, and correct instruction leaflet. Sold for £170, Vectis, October.

Dinky Toys No 941 Foden (2nd Type) 14-ton "Mobilgas" Tanker, red including Supertoy hubs with black treaded tyres, silver trim, metal gantry and tow hook. Good plus in good plus box with yellow "Hudson Dobson" label to side. Sold for £300, Vectis, October.

Dinky Toys No 949 Wayne School Bus, yellow body, black flashes and trim, red interior and plastic hubs with black treaded tyres. Good plus to excellent in good blue and white striped lift off lid box. Sold for £120, Vectis, October.

Dinky Toys No 979 Racehorse Transporter "Newmarket Racehorse Transport Service Ltd", two-tone grey, pale yellow including Supertoy hubs with black treaded tyres, silver trim, with 2 horse figures. Excellent plus in excellent box. Sold for £220, Vectis, October.

Dinky Toys No 101 Sunbeam Alpine Sports Car, turquoise body, dark blue interior with driver figure, silver trim, mid-blue ridged hubs with black smooth tyres. Excellent in good box. Sold for £160, Vectis, October.

Dinky Toys No 103 Austin Healey 100 Sports Car, cream body, red interior and ridged hubs with black treaded tyres, driver figure, silver trim. Excellent plus in good box. Sold for £160, Vectis, October.

Dinky Toys No 102 MG Midget Sports Car, yellow body, red interior, tonneau and ridged hubs with black smooth tyres, driver figure, silver trim. Excellent plus in good plus box. Sold for £170, Vectis, October.

Dinky Toys No 106 Austin Atlantic Convertible, pale blue, red interior, tonneau and ridged hubs with black smooth tyres, silver trim. Excellent plus in poor box. Sold for £60, Vectis, October.

Dinky Toys No 151 Triumph 1800 Saloon, dark blue, fawn ridged hubs with black smooth tyres, silver trim. Excellent in good box. Sold for £140, Vectis, October.

Dinky Toys No 170 Ford Fordor Sedan Low-line, two-tone pale cream, red including ridged hubs with black smooth tyres, silver trim. Good plus to excellent in good plus yellow and red carded picture box with correct colour spot. Sold for £70, Vectis, October.

Corgi Toys No 468 London Transport Routemaster Bus "Red Rose Tea", red body, cream interior, yellow plastic stairs, chrome spun hubs, silver grille with correct plastic figure. Near mint in good plus box with collectors club folded leaflet. Sold for £360, Vectis, October.

Corgi Toys No 448 BMC Mini "Police" Van, dark blue body, red interior, silver trim, grey plastic aerial, cast hubs, with tracker and dog figures. Near mint, box is good plus to excellent, with collectors club folded leaflet. Sold for £340, Vectis, October.

Corgi Toys No 98751 "Chitty Chitty Bang Bang" 1992 "25th Anniversary" issue, complete with correct certificate and folded leaflets. Near mint, box is mint. Sold for £130, Vectis, October.

Corgi Toys No 275 Rover 2000 TC, white body, amber roof panel, dark red interior, chrome trim, Golden Jacks take-off wheels. Good plus in good plus window box with pictorial header. Sold for £80, Vectis, October.

Tri-ang Spot-on No155 Austin FX4 "Taxi", black body, pale cream interior and steering wheel, silver trim, spun hubs. Good plus in good carded box, with collectors club folded leaflet. Sold for £60, Vectis, October.

Tri-ang Spot-on No 281 MG Midget Mk.II, red body, pale cream interior with red steering wheel (without driver figure), chrome trim and spun hubs. Good plus, unboxed. Sold for £50, Vectis, October.

Tri-ang Spot-on Land Rover, green body, silver base, grey interior with black steering wheel, spun hubs, tow hook. Excellent plus. Sold for £35, Vectis, October.

Taylor & Barrett Trolleybus, red body, black wheelarches and wheels, with poles. Good plus. Sold for £25, Vectis, October.

Charbens Tractor, yellow body with green and black figure, silver trim, metal wheels. Good. Sold for £30, Vectis, October.

Benbros (Mighty Midget Series) 15 Vespa Scooter, blue including metal wheels. Scooter is near mint with a good red and green figure driver in an excellent carded box. Sold for £110, Vectis, October.

Matchbox Superfast 53a Ford Zodiac, metallic green with unpainted base, narrow 5-spoke wheels and ivory interior. Good in excellent plus "New" Type G Box with incorrect spelling to both end flaps "Ford Zodiak". Sold for £620, Vectis, October.

Matchbox Superfast 14a Iso Grifo empty box, rare type F colour picture box (without Superfast text). Excellent plus. Sold for £320, Vectis, October.

Matchbox Lesney large scale Horse Drawn Milk Float "The Perfect Toy", "Pasteurised Milk" in white, grey metal wheels, white driver figure, brown horse with white detailing, with 6 original white milk crates. Good plus, unboxed. Sold for £170, Vectis, October.

Corgi Toys No 224 Bentley Continental Sports Saloon carded display stand, appears never to have been set for display. Near mint. Sold for £600, Vectis, October.

Corgi Toys No 202m Morris Cowley Saloon, green body, silver trim, flat spun hubs, mechanical motor. Excellent plus in fair blue carded box. Sold for £60, Vectis, October.

Corgi Toys No 206m Hillman Husky, grey body, silver trim, flat spun hubs, mechanical motor. Excellent in poor to fair blue carded picture box. Sold for £110, Vectis, October.

Corgi Toys No 215 Ford Thunderbird Open Sports Car, white body, blue and silver interior, flat spun hubs. Excellent in good blue and yellow carded picture box. Sold for £80, Vectis, October.

Corgi Toys No 245 Chrysler Imperial, red body, pale blue interior with 2 figures, chrome trim and spun hubs, with golf bag and trolley. Good plus to excellent in good blue and yellow carded picture box. Sold for £180, Vectis, October.

Corgi Toys No 423 Bedford Utilicon Fire Tender "Fire Dept", red, silver trim, flat spun hubs, mechanical motor, black ladders. Good plus, but incorrect issue for fair blue and yellow carded No 423 box. Sold for £70, Vectis, October.

Corgi Toys No 300 Austin Healey Sports Car, red, cream seats, silver trim, flat spun hubs. Excellent in good to good plus blue carded picture box. Sold for £100, Vectis, October.

Corgi Toys No 304 Mercedes 300 SL Hardtop Roadster, yellow, red hood, silver trim, flat spun hubs. Good to good plus in good yellow and red carded picture box. Sold for £70, Vectis, October.

Dinky Toys Packard Super Eight Tourer (39a). Example in mid blue with smooth black wheels and white tyres, black base and thick axles so suggests an early post WW2 example. Very good, light chipping. Sold for £220, Wallis and Wallis, November.

Dinky Toys 39 Series Chrysler Royal sedan (39e). A scarce 1939 pre-WW2 example in dark green, with black smooth wheels and white tyres and silver painted base. Very good for age some light chipping. Sold for £170, Wallis and Wallis, November.

Dinky Toys 39 Series Chrysler Royal sedan (39e). A U.S. export example in tan, with red wings, tan ridged wheels with black tyres and black painted base. Good condition, some chipping. Sold for £380, Wallis and Wallis, November.

Dinky Toys 39 Series Lincoln Zephyr Coupe (39c). A U.S. export red with maroon wings, with red ridged wheels with black tyres and black crackle base. Good condition, some chipping. Sold for £300, Wallis and Wallis, November.

Dinky Toys 39 Series Oldsmobile 6 sedan (39b). A U.S. export, two tone blue, black tyres and black crackle base. Good condition some chipping. Sold for £260, Wallis and Wallis, November.

Dinky Toys 39 Series Chrysler Royal sedan (39e). A U.S. export, two tone green, black tyres and black painted base. Good condition some chipping. Sold for £220, Wallis and Wallis, November.

A scarce Dinky Toys 39 Series Oldsmobile 6 sedan (39b), an example in two tone U.S. export colours, cream and tan, with black painted base, black ridged wheels and black tyres. Mint condition, a couple of very small chips only. Sold for £420, Wallis and Wallis, November.

Dinky Supertoys No.501 Foden Diesel 8-Wheel Wagon. Early example in the first colour, dark brown with silver flash to cab, black chassis and mudguards, dark brown wheels with correct early herringbone tyres. In early utility style box with red/white applied labels, some wear overall. Very good condition, minor chipping only for age. Sold for £110, Wallis and Wallis, November.

Dinky Supertoys Foden FG Flat Truck (902) example with orange cab and chassis and green wheels and body. Boxed with USA sales label to lid, some wear/damage. Vehicle very good, very minor chipping in a few places. Sold for £110, Wallis and Wallis, November.

Dinky Supertoys Mighty Antar Transporter with Transformer (908). Yellow tractor unit, with grey flatbed and red wheels and ramps. Boxed, with inner packing pieces and instructions for assembling the Transformer, very minor wear. Very good to mint, minor chipping to hinge of ramps and connecting pin only. Sold for £380, Wallis and Wallis, November.

Corgi Toys Oldsmobile Super 88 (235). An example in light metallic steel blue with white flash and red interior, dished spun wheels and black tyres. Boxed, minor marking/sticker. Vehicle Mint. Sold for £110, Wallis and Wallis, November.

Corgi Toys Studebaker 'Golden Hawk' (211M). A scarce example in white with gold flash, mechanical motor in working order. Boxed, with range leaflet. Box has one inner flap missing. Vehicle mint. Sold for £300, Wallis and Wallis, November.

A Corgi Toys Commer Three Quarter Ton Van, an example in 'Hammonds' promotional livery, blue and white with green roof. Cast wheels. In un-numbered Corgi box with '462' handwritten to ends. Sold for £180, Wallis and Wallis, November.

Matchbox Gift Set G4. 'Team Matchbox Superfast Champions'. Comprising racing car transporter (K-7) in yellow, plus 4 single seater racing cars- 2 MB-24, Team Matchbox and 2 MB-34 Formula 1. Boxed, some wear/damage. Contents very good to mint, car sticker and badge missing. Sold for £130, Wallis and Wallis, November.

A Matchbox Series Ferrari Berlinetta (75b). In red with chrome wheels and black plastic tyres. Boxed. Vehicle very good to mint, very minor chip to raised edge of bonnet. Sold for £300, Wallis and Wallis, November.

A Matchbox Series Car Transporter gift set, (G-2) comprising; a Guy Warrior Car Transporter, Farnborough Measham (M8), a Jaguar Mk.10 in metallic bronze (28c), a Jaguar E type in metallic red (32b), a Rolls Royce Phantom V in light metallic mauve (44b), Mercedes Benz 220SE in dark red (53b). Boxed with inner yellow plastic tray, some wear and minor damage. Very good, minor chipping to all. Sold for £160, Wallis and Wallis, November.

Corgi Aviation Archive 1/72 scale (Nose Art Collection) US35304 B-25C Mitchell, "Oh-7" 445th Bombardment Squadron/321st Bombardment Group Oujda, French Morocco, January 1944. Near mint to mint in good plus to excellent outer pictorial lift off lid box complete with excellent inner plastic packaging. Sold for £70, Vectis, November.

Corgi Aviation Archive 1/72 scale US34014 (Nose Art Collection) B-24J Liberator 20 42-99813, "Sleepy Time Gal" 776th Bombardment Squadron/464th Bombardment Group, Pantanella, Italy, July 1945. Near mint to mint in good to good plus outer pictorial lift off lid box complete with inner polystyrene packaging. Sold for £80, Vectis, November.

Corgi Aviation Archive 1/72 scale US33308 (Nose Art Collection) B-17G Flying Fortress, "Mount n' Ride", 323rd Bombardment Squadron/91st Bombardment Group, Bassingbourn, April 1944. Near mint to mint in good to good plus box complete with inner polystyrene packaging. Sold for £140, Vectis, November.

Corgi Aviation Archive 1/32 scale US33906 (Flight Line Collection) Spitfire Mk.IA, Flight Sergeant George "Grumpy" Unwin, "Flash" and Ground Crew, No.19 Squadron, Duxford, 1940, with 4 1/32nd scale hand painted metal figures. Near mint to mint in good to good plus box along with inner polystyrene packaging. Sold for £110, Vectis, November.

Corgi Aviation Archive 1/32 scale US34405 (Flight Line Collection) P-51D Mustang, "Old Crow", Captain Clarence "Bud" Anderson and Ground Crew, 357th Fighter Group, Leiston, November 1944, with 4 1/32nd scale hand painted metal figures. Near mint to mint in good to good plus box complete with inner polystyrene packaging. Sold for £120, Vectis, November.

Corgi Aviation Archive 1/32 scale US35503 (Flight Line Collection) Hurricane Mk.I, P2923 No 85 Squadron, FLG. OFF. A. G. Lewis, Castle Camps, 1940, with 3 1/32nd scale hand painted metal figures. Near mint to mint in good to good plus box complete with inner polystyrene packaging. Sold for £110, Vectis, November.

Corgi Aviation Archive 1/32 scale AA33907 (Deluxe) Supermarine Spitfire Mk.1, ZP-A, No 74 Squadron, RAF, Flt Lt. Adolph "Sailor" Malan (1st Skirmish, Battle of Britain), with authentic engine sounds and replica cockpit controls. Near mint to mint in good to good plus box complete with inner polystyrene packaging. Sold for £100, Vectis, November.

Corgi Aviation Archive 1/32 scale AA34402 (World War II - Europe and Africa) P-51D-10-NA Mustang, "Old Crow" Captain Clarence "Bud" Anderson, 362nd FS, 357th FG, 1944. Near mint to mint in good to good plus box complete with inner polystyrene packaging. Sold for £50, Vectis, November.

Corgi Aviation Archive 1/32 scale (World War II - War in the Pacific) P-51D Mustang, "Stinger VII", Major Robert W. Moore 45th FS, 15th FG, Iwo Jima (South Field), June 1945. Near mint to mint in good box complete with inner polystyrene packaging. Sold for £45, Vectis, November.

Corgi Aviation Archive 1/72 scale set AA99127, Heinkel HE111H-3-2 Staffel (KG100, 1940-41), Messerschmitt ME109E-JG51 (Heinzbar, 1940), Supermarine Spitfire Mk.I X4253, 611 Squadron, P.O. Pegge, Rochford, 1940. Near mint to mint in good to good plus outer pictorial lift off lid box complete with inner polystyrene packaging. Sold for £80, Vectis, November.

Corgi Aviation Archive 1/72 scale AA32607 (World War II - Bombers on the Horizon) Avro Lancaster Mk.I, W4783, 'G' 460 Squadron, RAAF, Breighton Airfield, Yorkshire. Near mint to mint in good plus box complete with inner polystyrene packaging. Sold for £120, Vectis, November.

Corgi Aviation Archive No AA99126 "World War II - War in the Pacific" 8th Army Air Force 3-piece Set, Boeing B-17F - "Miss Minookie" (91st BG, 323rd BS), P47D Thunderbolt - "Rozzie Geth II"/"Miss Fire" (62nd FS, 56th FG) and P51D Mustang (375th FS, 361st FG). Near mint to mint in good to good plus box complete with inner polystyrene packaging. Sold for £80, Vectis, November.

Corgi Aviation Archive 1/72 scale (War in the Pacific) Boeing B-17G, 44-83514, Confederate Air Force, Arizona Wing, Mesa, Arizona. Flies as 483514, "Sentimental Journey". Near mint to mint in good plus to excellent box complete with inner polystyrene packaging. Sold for £150, Vectis, November.

Corgi Aviation Archive 1/32 scale (World War II - Fleet Air Arm) Hawker Sea Hurricane 1B, No 880 Squadron, Fleet Air Arm, HMS Indomitable, Indian Ocean, May 1942 (restored aircraft - The Shuttleworth Collection). Near mint to mint in good to good plus box complete with inner polystyrene packaging. Sold for £80, Vectis, November.

Corgi Aviation Archive 1/72 scale AA36904 Junkers JU52/3M, RJ+NP, C-Schulen (Multi-engine Flying School), Thorn, (Eastern Front December 1941). Near mint to mint in good plus to excellent box, with a good to good plus outer cardboard slip sleeve. Sold for £110, Vectis, November.

Corgi Aviation Archive 1/72 scale AA34015 Consolidated B-24H Liberator, 756th BS/459th BG, Giulia Field, Cerignola, Italy, late 1944. Near mint to mint in good plus to excellent outer box, with good to good plus outer cardboard slip sleeve. Sold for £130, Vectis, November.

Corgi Aviation Archive 1/72 scale AA32616 Lancaster B1 Day Bomber (Grand Slam), 617th Sqn Y Z-J-U Boats Pens Raid at Farge, Germany, March 1945. Near mint to mint in good plus to excellent box. Sold for £130, Vectis, November.

Corgi Aviation Archive 1/72nd scale AA38601 BAC TSR-2, XR219, "The Only Prototype to Fly", 1964. Near mint to mint in good to good plus box complete with inner plastic packaging. Sold for £70, Vectis, November.

Corgi Aviation Archive 1/72 scale AA34707 English Electric Canberra TT.18, Royal Navy, Fleet Requirements Air Direction Unit, RNAS Yeovilton, Somerset 1985. Near mint to mint in good to good plus outer box complete with inner plastic packaging, with good to good plus outer cardboard slip sleeve. Sold for £100, Vectis, November.

Dinky Supertoys No 923 Big Bedford "Heinz 57 Varieties", red cab and chassis, yellow back with sauce bottle decal, Supertoy hubs and grey treaded tyres. Good plus in good box. Sold for £230, Warwick & Warwick, November.

Dinky Toys No 434 Bedford TK Crash Tender Top Rank Motorway Service, white cab, blue interior, Top Rank decals and dark green plastic hubs. Good plus in good box. Sold for £65, Warwick & Warwick, November.

Dinky Supertoys No 918 Guy Ever Ready Batteries For Life, blue, silver trim, red Supertoy hubs and black tyres. Good plus in good plus box. Sold for £110, Warwick & Warwick, November.

Dinky Toys No 952 Luxury Coach Vega Major, with battery operated side indicators, ivory body on rare metallic blue base and cast hubs along with blue interior. Good in good outer box. Sold for £45, Vectis, November.

Dinky Supertoys No 975 Ruston Bucyrus Excavator, yellow body, green jib and bucket, red chassis and black rubber tracks. Good plus in good plus Supertoys box. Sold for £210, Warwick & Warwick, November.

Dinky Toys No 448 Chevrolet El Camino Pick-up, light blue, red interior, cream, silver trim, spun hubs and red trailers. Good plus in good plus box. Sold for £140, Warwick & Warwick, November.

Dinky Supertoys No 977 Commercial Servicing Platform Vehicle, cream cab and chassis, red jib, Supertoy hubs and plastic basket. Excellent in good plus box. Sold for £160, Warwick & Warwick, November.

Corgi Toys No 1127 Simon Snorkel Fire Engine, red with figures. Good plus in good plus to excellent box. Sold for £40, Vectis, November.

Corgi Toys No 302 Hillman Hunter London to Sydney Marathon Winner, Decals applied, complete with kangaroo figure. Excellent in excellent window box. Sold for £120, Warwick & Warwick, November.

Dinky Supertoys No 501 Foden Diesel 8-wheel Wagon, grey cab and back, black chassis, red flashes and ridged hubs, grey tyres, silver trim. Good in good box. Sold for £40, Warwick & Warwick, November.

Dinky Supertoys No 986 Mighty Antar Low Loader with Propeller, red cab, grey Supertoy hubs, driver figure, light grey and black trailer with elastic straps and propeller load. Good plus in good plus box. Sold for £130, Warwick & Warwick, November.

Dinky Supertoys No 908 Mighty Antar with Transformer, yellow cab, red hubs with windows and driver figure, silver trim, grey trailer, red ramps and hubs, complete and transformer load. Good plus in good plus box with inner pieces (without instructions). Sold for £500, Warwick & Warwick, November.

Corgi Toys GS31 The 'Riviera' Gift Set, Buick Riviera, red trailer, blue boat with white hull, with captain, water skier and board. Excellent in good plus box and excellent inner plinth. Sold for £180, Warwick & Warwick, November.

Dinky Supertoys No 504 Foden 14 ton Tanker, red cab/chassis/ hubs, fawn tank, silver flash. Good plus in good plus blue Supertoys box. Sold for £160, Warwick & Warwick, November.

Fun Ho! Toys (New Zealand) Dealers Trade Box, 6 cast metal Austin Healey models in yellow, red, green and blue. Near mint in excellent trade box. Sold for £70, Vectis, December.

Corgi Toys No 300 Austin Healey Sports Car, scarce later production example in dark red, with cream seats, spun convex hubs. Near mint in good box with foldout leaflet. Sold for £360, Vectis, December.

Corgi Toys No 300 Austin Healey Sports Car, scarce colour variation of greyish-blue, with red interior seating, flat spun hubs, hand applied detail to the front and rear, fitted with smooth tyres and bare metal steering wheel. Good plus to excellent in excellent box. Sold for £2500, Vectis, December.

Corgi Toys No 219 Plymouth Sports Suburban Station Wagon, cream body with silver side stripe, tan roof, red interior, rare ivory base, flat spun hubs. Excellent plus in excellent blue/yellow box. Sold for £80, Vectis, December.

Corgi Toys No 226 Morris Mini Minor, metallic maroon body & base, lemon yellow interior, cast hubs. Excellent to excellent plus in good plus blue/yellow box. Sold for £45, Vectis, December.

Corgi Toys No 156 Cooper Maserati Formula 1 Racing Car, dark blue body with racing number 7 decals, bare metal cast hubs. Good plus in excellent blue/yellow box. Sold for £50, Vectis, December.

Corgi Toys No 159 Cooper Maserati F1 Racing Car, yellow & white body with racing number 3 labels, white base, bare metal cast hubs. Excellent plus in excellent plus blue/yellow box. Sold for £30, Vectis, December.

Corgi Toys No 327 MGB GT, dark red body, light blue interior, mid grey base, wire wheels. Excellent in good plus blue/yellow box. Sold for £40, Vectis, December.

Corgi Toys No 406 Land Rover, metallic blue body with cream roof, flat spun hubs, with No 102 Rice's Pony Trailer in red with gloss black wings and base. Excellent in good blue box for Land Rover only. Sold for £50, Vectis, December.

Corgi Toys No 102 Rice's Pony Trailer, tan trailer with cream roof, metallic silver base, spun hubs complete with original plastic pony which has blue jacket. Trailer is near mint, pony is excellent, in excellent plus blue/yellow box. Sold for £40, Vectis, December.

Corgi Toys No 408 Bedford CA AA Road Service Van, mustard yellow body with black front & roof, flat spun hubs. Excellent in good blue box. Sold for £50, Vectis, December.

Corgi Toys No 434 Volkswagen Transporter Kombi, two-tone metallic apple green lower body, very pale green upper body, red interior, light grey base, spun hubs. Excellent plus in fair blue/yellow box. Sold for £80, Vectis, December.

Corgi Toys No 438 Land Rover, metallic green body with olive green plastic rear canopy, lemon yellow interior, light grey base with silver plastic rear tow hook, cast hubs. Near mint in good box. Sold for £50, Vectis, December.

Corgi Toys No 438 Land Rover, metallic green body with olive green plastic rear canopy, lemon yellow interior, light grey base without tow hook fitted, cast hubs. Mint in excellent scarce late issue blue/yellow window box. Sold for £80, Vectis, December.

Corgi Toys GS7 Daktari Gift Set, sea green Land Rover with black stripes, lemon yellow interior, mid grey base, spun hubs, with figures of Doctor Marsh, Judy the Chimp, Clarence the Lion and Tiger. Excellent in good window box. Sold for £80, Vectis, December.

Dinky Toys No 36e pre-war British Salmson 2-seater Sports Car with driver, two-tone green, black smooth hubs, driver with brown coat. Fair to good. Sold for £260, Vectis, December.

Dinky Toys No 24g pre-war Sports Tourer 4-seater, powder blue body with brown wings and criss-cross chassis, no side lights, solid tinplate windscreen, steering wheel, black smooth hubs with thin axles and original white tyres. Fair to good. Sold for £110, Vectis, December.

Dinky Toys No 24d pre-war Vogue Saloon, cream, with blue wings and criss-cross chassis, black smooth hubs, thin axles. Fair to good. Sold for £300, Vectis, December.

Dinky Toys No 24d pre-war Vogue Saloon, violet blue with black front wings and criss-cross chassis. Fair. Sold for £100, Vectis, December.

Dinky Toys No 34a Royal Air Mail Service Car, RAF blue with black smooth hubs and thin axles, white tyres. Fair to good. Sold for £110, Vectis, December.

Dinky Toys No 28b pre-war Type 2 Delivery Van "Seccotine", RAF blue, with black hubs and thin axles. Fair to good. Sold for £120, Vectis, December.

Dinky Toys No 28f pre-war Type 2 Delivery Van "Virol", yellow, with legible transfers, black smooth hubs with white tyres. Fair to good. Sold for £360, Vectis, December.

Dinky Toys No 23e pre-war Speed of the Wind Racing Car, powder blue, with black smooth hubs. Fair to good. Sold for £30, Vectis, December.

Dinky Toys No 60y pre-war Thompson Aircraft Tender, red, with black wings, 3 white rubber tyres, includes driver figure. Fair to good. Sold for £90, Vectis, December.

French Dinky Toys No 26 pre-war Bugatti Autorail Railcar, cream, with yellow sides, green plastic rollers. Good plus. Sold for £100, Vectis, December.

Dinky Toys No pre-war Set 152 "Light Tank Set", Light Tank with chain type tracks and aerial, and 35 Series Austin Staff Car with driver figure, with 7 soldier figures. Fair in fair card box with pictorial background to good display base. Sold for £80, Vectis, December.

Dinky Toys No 25m Bedford End Tipper, orange cab, body and chassis, green ridged hubs. Excellent plus to near mint. Sold for £600, Vectis, December.

Dinky Toys No Gift Set 125 "Fun A'hoy" set, comprising No 130 Ford Corsair in powder blue with off-white interior, orange Healey Boat Trailer with red/cream plastic boat and 2 figures. Excellent plus to near mint in excellent box. Sold for £220, Vectis, December.

Dinky Supertoys No 751 Lawn Mower, green/red. Excellent in excellent early blue box with orange and white label. Sold for £100, Vectis, December.

Dublo Dinky Toys No 073 Land Rover and Horse Trailer, comprising green Series 1 Land Rover with orange horse box trailer and plastic horse figure to interior. Excellent to near mint in good plus box. Sold for £110, Vectis, December.

Dinky Toys No 140 Morris 1100, sky blue body, red interior, spun hubs. Excellent in good yellow/red box. Sold for £80, Vectis, December.

Corgi Toys GS15 Silverstone Racing Layout Gift Set, seven vehicles, all good plus to excellent in fair to good plus boxes, five kits unmade in original factory plastic bags complete with instructions & unused decal sheets, plus figure packs. Good to near mint in fair to good boxes. Sold for £1700, Vectis, December.

Dinky Toys No 39c pre-war Lincoln Zephyr Coupe, mid-green, with black smooth hubs, thin axles and lacquered baseplate, lacks the front tyres and some play wear. Fair to good. Sold for £320, Vectis, December.

Dinky Toys No39e pre-war Chrysler Royal Sedan, scarce yellow example, with black smooth hubs, thin axles and lacquered baseplate, some play wear. Fair to good. Sold for £680, Vectis, December.

Dinky Toys No 39f pre-war Studebaker Stake Commander 2-door Coupe, violet blue with black smooth hubs, thin axles and lacquered baseplate, lacks a rear tyre. Fair to good. Sold for £580, Vectis, December.

Dinky Toys No 264 Ford Fairlane RCMP Patrol Car, dark navy blue body with white door panels, red roof-light & original rear aerial, ivory interior complete with both figures, baseplate without number cast, spun hubs. Excellent plus in good box. Sold for £320, Vectis, December.

Dinky Toys No 920 Guy Warrior Van "Heinz Tomato Ketchup", red cab & chassis, yellow van body & Supertoy hubs, signs of some repainting to van body roof although both decals are factory original. Excellent in good plus correct blue-striped box. Sold for £660, Vectis, December.

Dinky Toys No 109 Austin Healey 100 in competition finish, mustard yellow, with black knobbly tyres, racing number 28, white driver and blue interior with ridged hubs. Excellent in good box. Sold for £440, Vectis, December.

Tri-ang Spot-on No 105 Austin Healey, scarce colour variation of dark grey, with white interior. Near mint in good box with picture card (depicting the two-tone colour scheme). Sold for £220, Vectis, December.

Tootsietoy (USA) Austin Healey Cars, kit with bare metal diecast body, wheels and other fittings, plus pair of unboxed No 24 cars in blue and bronze. Kit is excellent including backing card and blister pack, loose cars are fair to good. Sold for £45, Vectis, December.

Dinky Toys No 23a post-war Racing Car, silver with red trim, racing number 4, black ridged hubs. Excellent plus. Sold for £35, Vectis, December.

Dinky Toys No 35d Austin 7 Open Tourer, light blue with black solid wheels, this version not fitted with wire windscreen. Excellent. Sold for £50, Vectis, December.

Dinky Toys No 30b post-war Rolls-Royce, scarce very dark blue with black solid chassis and ridged hubs. Excellent plus. Sold for £110, Vectis, December.

Dinky Toys Salmson 4-seater, fawn with black wings and ridged hubs, solid tinplate windscreen. Excellent plus. Sold for £200, Vectis, December.

Dinky Toys No 102 MG Midget, lime green body with cream interior & driver, beige ridged hubs. Excellent plus in good box with correct colour spot. Sold for £130, Vectis, December.

Dinky Toys No 192 Range Rover, metallic bronze body, light blue interior, bare metal base, cast hubs. Mint in good plus box. Sold for £45, Vectis, December.

Dinky Toys No 475 1908 Ford Model T, dark blue body, gloss black chassis, brown plastic wheels, complete with original figures. Mint in good plus window box. Sold for £20, Vectis, December.

Dinky Toys No 252 Bedford Refuse Truck, orange cab & chassis, light grey rear body with mid-green rear opening hatch, darker green plastic rear shutters with windows fitted, silver painted radiator grille & headlamps, gloss black tinplate base, red plastic hubs with black treaded tyres. Excellent in good lighter yellow box. Sold for £220, Vectis, December.

Dinky Toys No 563 Blaw Knox Heavy Tractor, burnt orange body complete with tan driver, mid-green rollers with original & pliable olive green rubber tracks. Excellent plus in excellent box. Sold for £90, Vectis, December.

Corgi Toys No 422 Bedford CA Van "Corgi Toys", yellow body with single windscreen, mid-blue ribbed roof, flat spun hubs. Good. Sold for £45, Vectis, December.

Dinky Toys No 253 Daimler Ambulance, white body, with windows fitted, gloss black baseplate with model number 253, cherry red ridged wheels. Excellent in good to good plus box. Sold for £40, Vectis, December.

Dinky Toys No 257 Nash Rambler Fire Chief's Car, red body with red roof light, matt black base, spun hubs. Excellent plus in good plus to excellent box. Sold for £70, Vectis, December.

Dinky Toys (Made in Hong Kong) No 57/001 Buick Riviera, light blue body with ivory roof, red interior, matt black base. Excellent plus in fair box. Sold for £90, Vectis, December.

Dinky Toys (Made in Hong Kong) No 57/005 Ford Thunderbird Hardtop, mid-blue body with white roof, red interior, matt black base. Excellent to excellent plus in good plus to excellent box. Sold for £190, Vectis, December.

Dinky Toys (Made in Hong Kong) No 57/006 Rambler Classic Station Wagon, green body with silver rear roof panel, ivory interior, matt black base. Near mint in good plus box. Sold for £150, Vectis, December.

Dinky Toys No 117 Four Berth Caravan, yellow body with pale grey plastic opening door, large roof window panel, red interior with blue carpet, matt black baseplate, spun hubs, knobbly grey plastic jockey wheel. Excellent to excellent plus in fair box. Sold for £100, Vectis, December.

Dinky Toys No 27D/340 Land Rover, burnt orange body, dark blue interior complete with tan driver, red ridged wheels with grey tyres. Good plus in fair trade box Sold for £60, Vectis, December.

Dinky Toys No 176 Austin A105 Westminster Saloon, light grey body & roof with red side stripes, gloss black baseplate, spun hubs with white treaded tyres. Excellent unboxed. Sold for £50, Vectis, December.

Dinky Toys No 289 London Transport Routemaster Bus "Tern Shirts", red body with cream lower deck seats, ivory upper deck seats, complete with driver & clippie figures, spun hubs. Good plus in good to good plus box. Sold for £20, Vectis, December.

Dinky Toys No 29G/281 Luxury Coach, beige body with burnt orange wings & side stripes, beige ridged wheels. Excellent in good dual-numbered box. Sold for £90, Vectis, December.

Dinky Toys No 219 Big Cat Jaguar XJ12 Coupe, white body with red & black labels, black interior, black plastic base, chrome plastic wheels. Near mint in excellent plus to near mint reproduction window box. Sold for £60, Vectis, December.

French Dinky Toys No 546 Austin Healey 100, white body, matt red interior with cream steering wheel & driver, original windscreen, spun hubs. Excellent plus in good box. Sold for £50, Vectis, December.

French Dinky Toys No 33AN Simca Cargo "Bailly", yellow cab & rear body with white roof, yellow ridged wheels. Excellent plus in good box. Sold for £110, Vectis, December.

French Dinky Toys No 811 Caravan, cream body with red side stripes & white roof, chrome ridged wheels. Excellent to excellent plus in good box. Sold for £70, Vectis, December.

Dinky Toys No 360 Gerry Anderson's Space:1999 Eagle Freighter, metallic blue with white body, red thrusters on moon polystyrene inner tray. Mint with unapplied decals in excellent box. Sold for £210, Warwick & Warwick, January.

Matchbox Moko Lesney Prime Mover, orange cab, blue trailer plus yellow and red bulldozer with green tracks. Good plus in good box. Sold for £310, Warwick & Warwick, January.

Corgi Toys GS27 Bedford TK Machinery Carrier and Priestman Cub Shovel plus others, mid-blue machinery carrier with black and silver trailer and standard Cub Shovel, plus No 57 Massey Ferguson 65 Tractor, No 480 Chevrolet Taxi, and No 472 Public Address Vehicle. Excellent in good or better boxes. Sold for £180, Warwick & Warwick, January.

Corgi Toys No 204M Rover 90 Saloon Car, with working flywheel motor, green body, flat spun wheel hubs. Mint in excellent box with two leaflets. Sold for £300, C&T Auctions, January.

Corgi Toys No 208M Jaguar 2.4 Litre Saloon Car, metallic blue body, with scarce grey base, flat spun wheels, with working mechanical mechanism. Near mint in excellent box, with two leaflets. Sold for £340, C&T Auctions. January.

Corgi Toys No 233 Heinkel Economy Car, scarce dark red body, silver trim, yellow interior, flat spun wheels. Mint in mint box, with Corgi Model Club TV21 leaflet. Sold for £190, C&T Auctions. January.

Corgi Toys No 238 Jaguar Mark X Saloon, pale blue body, silver trim, red interior, shaped spun wheels, luggage in boot. Mint in mint blue and yellow original picture box. Sold for £200, C&T Auctions. January.

Corgi Toys No 318 Lotus Elan S2, metallic blue, driver, spun wheel hubs, "I've got a tiger in my tank" decal on boot, racing number 2 decal sheet. Mint in mint original blue/yellow picture box, with inner packing piece. Sold for £320, C&T Auctions. January.

Corgi Toys No 419 Ford Zephyr Police Motorway Patrol, white body, silver trim, red interior, shaped spun wheels, aerial, large roof light. Mint in mint box, with white inner card packing piece and Corgi Model Club leaflet. Sold for £260, C&T Auctions. January.

Corgi Toys No 430 Ford Thunderbird Bermuda Taxi, white body, silver trim, green/red canopy, with driver, shaped spun wheel hubs. Mini in mint yellow/blue picture box, with inner card packing ring. Sold for £220, C&T Auctions. January.

Corgi Toys No 481 Chevrolet Impala Police Car, white/black body, chrome plated bumpers/side strip, lemon interior, cast wheel hubs, two policeman figures"Police Patrol" labels. Mint in excellent blue/yellow illustrated box, with correct inner packing and Corgi leaflet. Sold for £220, C&T Auctions. January.

Corgi Major Toys No 1135 Bedford TK Military Heavy Equipment Transporter, USA star, with driver, olive military green body, yellow interior, shaped spun wheels. Mint on excellent inner card tray, with scarce white inner card packing, in excellent blue/yellow illustrated box. Sold for £600, C&T Auctions. January.

Corgi Toys Gift Set No 9 Massey Ferguson 165 Tractor with shovel and tipping trailer, red/silver tractor and red/yellow trailer, with detachable raves. Mint in excellent yellow/blue illustrated box, mint inner display card stand, two white inner packing pieces and TV 21 Corgi Model Club leaflet. Sold for £380, C&T Auctions. January.

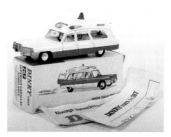

Dinky Toys No 267 Superior Cadillac Ambulance, red/white body, battery operated flashing light, with stretcher and patient. Mint in near mint box, with inner packing ring, instruction leaflet, and Dinky promotional leaflet. Sold for £170, C&T Auctions. January.

Dinky Supertoys 948 Tractor-Trailer Mclean USA Promotional Model 'Brown Shoe Co.', red cab, light grey trailer and red plastic hubs, with Brown Shoe St Louis labels applied to cab and rear trailer. Very good in excellent blue and white striped picture box. Sold for £3300, C&T Auctions. January.

Tri-ang Spot On No 107 Jaguar XKSS, scarce orange body, white interior/hood. Excellent to near mint in excellent picture card box. Sold for £980, C&T Auctions. January.

Dinky Toys Pre-War Set No 44 A.A. Hut Motorcycle Patrol and Guides, AA tinplate box with three signs, motorcycle patrol, AA guide directing traffic and AA guide saluting. Very good to excellent in fair to good blue lidded box with original card insert. Sold for £300, C&T Auctions. January.

Dinky Toys No 788 Six Buckets for Marrel Multi Bucket unit, light grey skip buckets. Mint in excellent yellow trade box with card dividers. Sold for £180, C&T Auctions. January.

Tri-ang Spot On No 102 Bentley 4 Door Sports Saloon, metallic blue over silver body, white interior. Near mint in very good to excellent box, with technical data picture sheet and Fleet Owners Club leaflet. Sold for £280, C&T Auctions. January.

Tekno (Denmark) No 830 Volvo 121 Station Wagon, beige body, red interior, chrome wheel hubs. Mint in mint box. Sold for £200, C&T Auctions. January.

Dinky Toys No 25J 6x Civilian Jeeps in trade box, 2 blue/yellow wheel hubs, 2 red/blue wheel hubs and 2 light green/red wheel hubs. Near mint in good yellow trade box is good, with card dividers. Sold for £620, C&T Auctions. January.

Dinky Toys No 920 Guy Warrior Heinz Van, red cab/chassis, yellow back/wheel hubs, window glazing, "HEINZ 57 VARIETIES" with Tomato Ketchup Bottle advertising. Near mint in very good blue/white stripe box. Sold for £1500, C&T Auctions. January.

Tri-ang Spot On No 102 Bentley 4 Door Sports Saloon, red/cream body, cream interior. Excellent in very good to excellent box, with correct colour spot and Fleet Owners Club leaflet. Sold for £280, C&T Auctions. January.

Dinky Supertoys No 908 Mighty Antar with Transformer, dark yellow tractor unit, grey trailer, rare yellow diecast wheel hubs, red ramps, transformer containing sealed parts and instructions. Excellent in good to excellent box, with inner packing pieces. Sold for £2800, C&T Auctions. January.

Dinky Toys No 251 Aveling Barford Diesel Roller, scarce lime green body, red rollers, tan driver. Mint in very good yellow/red box with inner card packing. Sold for £500, C&T Auctions. January.

Dinky Supertoys No 935 Leyland Octopus Flat Truck With Chains, dark blue cab/chassis, pale yellow flash around cab and front bumper, light grey flatbed/plastic wheel hubs. Very good to excellent in excellent box, with correct blue colour spot. Sold for £8200, C&T Auctions. January.

Tri-ang Spot On No 105 Austin Healey "100-SIX", turquoise body, red interior. Excellent to near mint in very good to excellent box. Sold for £580, C&T Auctions. January.

Dinky Toys 989 No Auto Transporter (Car Carrier), rare USA Export issue, pale yellow cab, pale grey back, blue ramps, red plastic wheel hubs 'Auto Transporters'. Near mint in fair to good original export only gold window display box. Sold for £1200, C&T Auctions. January.

Dinky Toys Superfast Gift Set 245, No 131 Jaguar E Type, white body, gold base, spoked wheels, No 153 Aston Martin DB6, metallic silver blue, spoked wheels and No188 Jensen FF, yellow body, cast wheels. Near mint to mint in good window display box. Sold for £280, C&T Auctions. January.

Tekno (Denmark) No 824 MGA 1600, red body, white interior, cast wheel hubs. Mint in mint box. Sold for £130, C&T Auctions. January.

Tekno (Denmark) No 925 Mercedes Benz 300 SL Hardtop, red body, black hardtop white interior, chrome wheel hubs. Mint in mint box. Sold for £120, C&T Auctions. January.

Tekno 0302 Mercedes Benz Single Deck Coach, blue/cream body, cast wheel hubs, tan seats. Excellent to near mint in very good illustrated box. Sold for £60, C&T Auctions. January.

Tri-ang Spot-On No 100 Ford Zodiac, grey over light blue body, red interior. Very good in fair to good box, with correct colour spot. Sold for £170, C&T Auctions. January.

Matchbox Lesney King Size K-20 Ford D800 Tractor Transporter, red cab/trailer/plastic wheel hubs, yellow petrol tank, three blue/yellow Ford tractors. Mint in excellent unpunched header card window box. Sold for £180, C&T Auctions. January.

Matchbox Kingsize K-13 ERF Ready Mix concrete truck, orange body, red plastic wheel hubs. Good to excellent in excellent window display box. Sold for £50, C&T Auctions. January.

Matchbox Kingsize K-10 Aveling-Barford Tractor Shovel, sea green body, maroon seats/steering wheel, red plastic wheel hubs, without air filter. Near mint in good illustrated box. Sold for £40, C&T Auctions. January.

Matchbox Kingsize K-9 CLAAS Combine Harvester, green body, red blades/wheel hubs. Near mint in near mint box. Sold for £50, C&T Auctions. January.

Matchbox Lesney King Size K-1 Foden Tipper Truck "Hoveringham", red cab/chassis, orange tipper, white suspension. Mint in mint window display box, with punched header card. Sold for £60, C&T Auctions. January.

Dinky Toys No 924 Aveling-Barford 'Centaur' Dump Truck, red and yellow, red plastic wheel hubs, white interior. Mint in mint box, with inner packing and small warning leaflet. Sold for £75, C&T Auctions. January.

Dinky Toys No 925 Leyland Dump Truck with Tilt Cab, white tilting cab and chassis, blue cab roof, orange tipper, white plastic tailgate, light blue interior, mid-blue plastic wheel hubs. Excellent to mint in good box. Sold for £135, C&T Auctions. January.

Dinky Supertoys No 930 Bedford Pallet Jekta Van, orange and yellow body, yellow hubs, "DINKY TOYS" and "MECCANO" adverts, yellow hubs, three pallets. Near mint in good to excellent blue and white striped box with inner packing and instructions. Sold for £240, C&T Auctions. January.

Dinky Toys No 932 Comet Wagon with Hinged Tailboard, dark green cab/chassis, orange back, cream ridged wheel hubs. Mint in excellent blue/white striped box. Sold for £220, C&T Auctions. January.

Dinky Supertoys No 965 Euclid Rear Dump Truck, with windows, "Stone-Ore-Earth" red-backed logo, pale yellow body/wheel hubs. Near mint in very good box, with one internal packing piece. Sold for £60, C&T Auctions. January.

Dinky Supertoys No 966 Albion Marrel Multi-Bucket Skip Lorry, pale yellow body, grey Marrell multi bucket unit, black plastic wheel hubs. Near mint in very good blue/white striped picture box, with inner card packing. Sold for £70, C&T Auctions. January.

Dinky Toys No 984 Atlas Digger, dark orange/yellow body, red interior, silver bucket, black tracks. Mint in good box, with inner packing card. Sold for £50, C&T Auctions. January.

Dinky Toys No 342 Austin Mini Moke, metallic green body, grey canopy, spun wheel hubs. Near mint in good box. Sold for £65, C&T Auctions. January.

Dinky Toys No 404 Conveyancer Fork Lift Truck, red/yellow, CG4 rear logo, with driver, red pallet, winding handle. Mint in excellent box, with instruction leaflet and inner packing. Sold for £50, C&T Auctions. January.

Dinky Toys No 726 Messerschmitt Bf 109E, olive green/yellow, sky blue. Mint on mint base but with poor bubble pack lid, with instructions and decal sheet. Sold for £130, C&T Auctions. January.

Dinky Toys No 734 P47 Thunderbolt, silver/black body, red four-blade propeller, with battery operated motor. Mint on mint base with excellent bubble pack lid, with decal sheet. Sold for £95, C&T Auctions. January.

Dinky Toys No 739 A6M5 Zero-Sen, metallic turquoise /black body, red three-blade propeller, with battery operated motor. Mint on mint base with mint bubble pack lid, with decal sheet. Sold for £120, C&T Auctions. January.

Dinky Toys 176 N.S.U. Ro 80, metallic dark red body, battery operated head & tail lights with luminous seats, spun wheel hubs. Near mint in excellent illustrated carded box and excellent inner card display, with instruction leaflet. Sold for £85, C&T Auctions. January.

Dinky Toys No 156 Saab 96, metallic red body, white interior, spun wheels. Near mint in fair illustrated carded box. Sold for £45, C&T Auctions. January.

Dinky Toys Sports Cars Gift Set 149 (Competition Finish), 108 M.G. Midget Sports, 109 Austin Healey 100 Sports, 107 Sunbeam Alpine Sports, 110 Aston Martin DB3S and 111 Triumph TR2 Sports, with racing drivers and numbers. Near mint in very good to excellent blue/white stripe box. Sold for £900, C&T Auctions. January.

Dinky Toys Pre-War No 62k The Kings Aeroplane, silver/red/ blue body 'G-A EXX', 2x 2-blade propellers. Excellent in good box. Sold for £110, C&T Auctions. January.

Dinky Toys Pre-War No 62g Boeing "Flying Fortress", silver body, 4x 4-blade propellers, USA Army Air Corps stars. Excellent in very good box. Sold for £75, C&T Auctions. January.

Dinky Toys No 30hm/624 Daimler Military Ambulance (USA Export issue), military green, red crosses on white backgrounds. Near mint, unboxed. Sold for £75, C&T Auctions. January.

Dinky Toys Pre-War No 37c Royal Signals Dispatch Rider, military green body, with white tyres. Good, but with some metal fatigue. Sold for £95, C&T Auctions. January.

Corgi Toys No 255 Austin A60 Motor School Car (Export Version), darker blue body, left hand drive, red interior, shaped spun wheels. Mint in mint blue picture box, with multi-language leaflet. Sold for £170, C&T Auctions. January.

Corgi Toys No 447 Walls Ice Cream Van on Ford Thames, blue/cream body, salesman figure, spun shaped wheel hubs, decals applied. Near mint, unboxed. Sold for £60, C&T Auctions. January.

Corgi Toys No 447 Walls Ice Cream Van on Ford Thames, blue/ cream body, salesman and boy figures, spun shaped wheel hubs, unapplied self-adhesive decal sheet. Near mint on excellent inner plinth in good blue/yellow box, with correct special Corgi Club leaflet/ instructions. Sold for £260, C&T Auctions. January.

Corgi Toys No 9004 "The World of Wooster" 1927 3-Litre Bentley, green, with figures of Bertie Wooster and Jeeves. Mint on good blister bubble pack with card insert, plus leaflet. Sold for £60, C&T Auctions. January.

Corgi Toys No 479 Commer Mobile Camera Van, "Samuelson Film Service Ltd", metallic blue/ white body, blue interior, shaped spun wheel hubs with cameraman, suitcase. Mint in very good window display box with no creasing to header card, plus TV21 Corgi Model Club leaflet. Sold for £220, C&T Auctions. January.

DIECAST   RAILWAYS   TOY FIGURES   TINPLATE   TV & FILM   OTHERS   EBUYS

Corgi Major Toys No 1146 Carrimore Tri-Deck MK.V Car Transporter with Scammell Handyman Mk3 Tractor Unit, orange/white/blue, with detachable loading ramp, red interior, cast wheel hubs. Mint in good blue/ yellow window display box, with correct instruction sheet and Corgi leaflet. Sold for £180, C&T Auctions. January.

Corgi Major Toys No 1153 Priestman Boom Crane, red/orange body, "Hi grab" operating boom. Mint on excellent, polystyrene inner in very good 1st issue blue/ yellow window box, with correct instruction sheet and Corgi leaflet. Sold for £60, C&T Auctions. January.

Corgi Toys Gift Set 10 Tank Transporter and Centurion Mk.III Tank, military green Mack transporter, camouflaged tank. Near mint in good box, with inner card packing and missiles still on sprue. Sold for £65, C&T Auctions. January.

Dinky Toys 989 No Auto Transporter (Car Carrier), rare USA Export issue, pale yellow cab, pale grey back, blue ramps, red plastic wheel hubs 'Auto Transporters'. Near mint in fair to good original export only gold window display box. Sold for £1200, C&T Auctions, January.

Corgi Toys 204M Rover 90 Saloon Car, with working flywheel motor, green body, flat spun wheel hubs, model is in mint original condition, early blue box is in excellent original condition, 3/11-price in pencil on one end flap, original concertina leaflet, pink Corgi club leaflet. Sold for £300, C&T Auctioneers, January.

Corgi Toys 208M Jaguar 2.4 Litre Saloon Car metallic blue body, with scarce grey base plate, flat spun wheels, in near mint original condition, with working mechanical mechanism, original early blue box is excellent, with all end flaps, original concertina leaflet, pink Corgi club leaflet. Sold for £340, C&T Auctioneers, January.

Corgi Toys 208 Jaguar 2.4 Litre Saloon Car, white body, flat spun wheels, in near mint original condition, with a mint original 208S blue/yellow picture box, with 208 A labels to end flaps, 3/8 price on one end flap, a nice bright example, one tiny paint chip to front bumper. Sold for £100, C&T Auctioneers, January.

Corgi Toys 210 Citroen D.S.19 metallic dark green body, black roof, silver base, flat spun wheels, in mint original condition, original early blue box is near mint, 3/6 in pencil to one end flap, original concertina leaflet, pink Corgi club leaflet. Sold for £200, C&T Auctioneers, January.

Corgi Toys 221 "Chevrolet" New York Taxi Cab, yellow body, red interior, aerial, flat spun wheel hubs, in near mint original condition, with an excellent original blue/yellow picture box, USA Salt Lake City vintage price label to one end flap, one slight crease to one picture side, Corgi model club leaflet. Sold for £260, C&T Auctioneers, January.

Corgi Toys 233 Heinkel Economy Car, red body, silver trim, yellow interior, flat spun wheels, in mint original condition, with a mint blue and yellow original illustrated box. Corgi model club TV21 leaflet. Sold for £110, C&T Auctioneers, January.

Scarce Corgi Toys 252 Rover 2000, with Trans-O-Lite headlamps, metallic maroon body, cream interior, shaped spun wheels, in mint original condition, blue/ yellow picture box is excellent, 5/6 in pencil on one end flap, with Corgi model club TV21 leaflet. Sold for £200, C&T Auctioneers, January.

Corgi Toys 238 Jaguar Mark X Saloon, pale blue body, silver trim, red interior, shaped spun wheels, luggage in boot, in mint original condition, with a mint blue and yellow original picture box, vintage USA 2.00 price label to one end flap. Sold for £200, C&T Auctioneers, January.

Corgi Toys 303 Mercedes-Benz 300SL Open Roadster, pale blue body, white interior, flat spun wheel hubs, in mint original condition, early blue box is in excellent original condition, 3/6 in pencil on one end flap, with an early pink Corgi club leaflet. Sold for £260, C&T Auctioneers, January.

Corgi Toys 318 Lotus Elan S2 metallic blue, driver, spun wheel hubs 'Ive got a tiger in my tank' decal on boot, with inner card packing, racing number 2 decal sheet, Corgi club leaflet, in mint original condition, with a mint original blue/yellow picture box. Sold for £320, C&T Auctioneers, January.

Brooklin Collection BRK 203 1961 Ford Galaxie Starliner 2-Door Hardtop. In 'Cambridge Blue Poly'. With light metallic blue interior, boxed, vehicle mint. Sold for £55, Wallis & Wallis, February.

Brooklin Collection BRK 145a. 1959 Chevrolet Brookwood Four Door Station Wagon. In 'Classic Cream' with tan interior, boxed, mint. Sold for £60, Wallis & Wallis, February.

Brooklin BRK93x 1935 Studebaker Commander Roadster. A C.T.C.S 2003 special in metallic silver with gold plated parts, black interior and black hood. A limited edition 1/250, boxed, mint. Sold for £65, Wallis & Wallis, February.

Brooklin BRK70x 1950 Dodge Wayfarer Coupe. A typical American 'Black & White' Police Car, with 2 sirens/lights to roof. An S.F.B.B.C. 1999 limited edition special, 1/200 produced, boxed, mint. Sold for £65, Wallis & Wallis, February.

Brooklin BRK108x 1957 Ford Ranchero. S.F.B.B.C. 2005 special. In light grey with dark grey interior, with grape basket load, in the livery of V. Sattui Winery. A limited edition 1/150, boxed, mint. Sold for £70, Wallis & Wallis, February.

Brooklin BRK82x 1959 De Soto Adventurer. A B.C.C. special 2005. In white with gold flash and wheels, with beige interior. A limited edition 1/200 produced, boxed, mint. Sold for £75, Wallis & Wallis, February.

Brooklin BRK87x 1949 Desoto Station Wagon. C.T.C.S 2001 in cream with wood effect to sides, 'Topley Taxi' with light brown interior. limited edition 1/275, boxed, mint. Sold for £70, Wallis & Wallis, February.

Brooklin BRK42x 1952 Ford Ranger minivan in dark brown Yosemite National Park livery, with maroon interior. S.F.B.B.C limited edition 1/200, boxed, mint. Sold for £60, Wallis & Wallis, February.

Brooklin 1958 Pontiac Bonneville Sport Coupe Hardtop. In pale pink with silver grey roof with cream/star side flash, with silver grey interior. An 8th Anniversary Club Model 1996, 1/350, boxed, mint. Sold for £65, Wallis & Wallis, February.

Brooklin Models BRK 53X. A 1956 Chevrolet Cameo Pick-Up. W.M.T.C. 1995. In mustard yellow with black interior and white-wall tyres, boxed, mint. Sold for £60, Wallis & Wallis, February.

Brooklin Models BRK56x 1965 Ford Mustang Convertible. W.M.T.C. 1997 limited edition model. In black with red interior, white tonneau, with mechanic figure. Boxed, mint. Sold for £70, Wallis & Wallis, February.

Brooklin Models BRK115x 1961 Airstream Bambi Caravan Trailer. 40th Anniversary Model Limited Edition B.C.C. Club Members Model. An example in metallic cerise, with silver fittings. Boxed, mint. Sold for £50, Wallis & Wallis, February.

Brooklin Models 1947 Dodge Series 21 Tow Truck C.T.C.S. 25th Anniversary model. In black and red livery, with beige interior. Together with a separate crane attachment. Boxed, vehicle mint. Sold for £65, Wallis & Wallis, February.

Brooklin Models BRK53x 1955 Chevrolet Cameo Carrier Pick-Up 'Franciscan Restaurant' S.F.B.B.C. 1996', 1/200/ In mid green with brown interior and silver box body. Boxed. Mint. Sold for £65, Wallis & Wallis, February.

Brooklin Models BRK61x 1960 Chevrolet Impala Convertible 'Mel's Drive In 50th Anniversary S.F.B.B.C. 1997'. In metallic maroon with cream interior, with driver, waitress and sign together with a card history of the diner. Boxed. Mint. Sold for £80, Wallis & Wallis, February.

Dinky Toys No 357 Klingon Battle Cruiser, from the TV series "Star Trek", original shrink wrapped factory trade pack of 6 examples. Mint in near mint to mint window boxes. Sold for £560, Vectis, February.

Dinky Toys pre-war Gift Set No 23 "Racing Cars", comprising red Auto Union Racer with black smooth hubs and racing number 1, yellow Mercedes-Benz Racing Car with black smooth hubs and racing number 1, powder blue Speed of the Wind Racing Car with black smooth hubs and racing number 1. Good to good plus in original light blue gift set box. Sold for £800, Vectis, February.

Tri-ang Spot-On 11/3 AEC Mammoth Major 8 with Flat Float, red cab and back, silver chassis and inner back, cream interior with grey plastic steering wheel, silver trim, cast hubs. Good plus to excellent in good lift off lid box. Sold for £420, Vectis, February.

French Dinky No 507a Fourgon Peugeot J7 Depannage "Autoroutes", orange body, grey interior, red roof light, black plastic aerial, concave hubs, with correct accessories. Excellent plus, inner pictorial stand is good plus to excellent, in good carded picture box. Sold for £420, Vectis, February.

Dinky Toys No 139b/171 Hudson Commodore, two-tone blue and tan with ridged hubs and smooth black tyres, silver trim. Excellent in good plus red and yellow carded picture box. Sold for £340, Vectis, February.

Dinky Trade Pack (empty) for 6x No 675 Army Staff Car (139am), with "Hudson Dobson" label to one end. Fair to good, but without dividers. Sold for £1200, Vectis, February.

Dinky Toys dealers wooden and glass shop display cabinet, rarer variation with front loader, two sliding front doors and opaque glass rear - missing internal glass shelves, but with metal supports. Good plus. Sold for £500, Vectis, February.

Hobby Master 1/32 scale Diecast Douglas SBD Dauntless model, excellent condition, box very good some rubs. Sold for £95, C&T Auctioneers, March.

Scratch Built Boat working model of HMS Leeds castle P258, model is in good untested condition, approx. 70cm long. Sold for £95, C&T Auctioneers, March.

Scratch Built Boat model of HMS Sheffield D80 Cruiser. Model is in fair to good condition approx. 100cm long, untested. Sold for £140, C&T Auctioneers, March.

Minichamps 1/35 scale model M60A1 W/ERA Tank, 'Kuwait City 1991', excellent condition in polystyrene packed box. Sold for £85, C&T Auctioneers, March.

Minichamps 1/35 scale model Panzerkampfwagen VI Tiger I Tank, 'Late Version', excellent condition in polystyrene packed box. Sold for £140, C&T Auctioneers, March.

Minichamps 1/35 scale model Panzerkampfwagen VI Tiger I Tank, 'Russia 1944', excellent condition in polystyrene packed box. Sold for £160, C&T Auctioneers, March.

Dinky Toys pair of light aircraft, both ex-shop stock taken from factory trade packs of 6 examples - No 710 Beechcraft S35 Bonanza and No 715 Beechcraft C55 Baron. Near mint to mint in near mint to mint bubble packs. Sold for £70, Vectis, March.

Dinky Toys No 254 Police Range Rover, ex-shop stock taken from factory trade packs of 6 examples - light blue interior, bare metal base, cast hubs with rubber tyres. Near mint in near mint to mint bubble pack. Sold for £50, Vectis, March.

Dinky Toys No 439 Ford D800 Snowplough, ex-shop stock taken from factory trade pack of 6 examples - metallic silver-blue cab with white interior, duck egg blue tipper body, lemon yellow plough, bare metal chassis, cast hubs. Excellent in excellent bubble pack. Sold for £50, Vectis, March.

Dinky Toys No 609 US Army 105mm Howitzer with gun crew, ex-shop stock taken from factory trade pack of 6 examples - unusual matt khaki green body complete with figures. Mint in excellent bubble pack. Sold for £45, Vectis, March.

Dinky Toys No 656 Wehrmacht German Army 88mm Gun with Mobile Limbers, ex-shop stock taken from trade pack of 6 examples. Mint in near mint to mint bubble pack. Sold for £90, Vectis, March.

Dinky Toys No 677 Task Force Set, ex-shop stock taken from factory trade pack of 6 examples, comprising matt khaki green Alvis Stalwart, matt blue DUKW Amphibian, and matt desert sand Ferret Armoured Car. Mint in excellent plus to near mint bubble pack. Sold for £45, Vectis, March.

Dinky Toys No 619 Bren Gun Carrier with Anti-Tank Field Gun, ex-shop stock taken from factory trade pack of 6 examples, with both figures & unused decal sheet. Mint in near mint bubble pack. Sold for £70, Vectis, March.

Dinky Toys No 622 British Army Bren Gun Carrier, ex-shop stock taken from factory trade packs of 6 examples, with plastic figures & unused decal sheet. Mint in excellent plus bubble pack. Sold for £50, Vectis, March.

Corgi Toys No C271/1 "James Bond" Aston Martin, light metallic grey, with driver and 2 loose passenger figures and copyright slip. Mint in good plus window box. Sold for £35, Vectis, March.

Corgi Toys No 273 Rolls Royce Silver Shadow with Mulliner Park Ward body, metallic white over grey, violet blue interior with gold effect steering wheel, fitted with take-off wheels and Golden Jacks. Near mint in excellent window box. Sold for £90, Vectis, March.

Corgi Toys No 302 Hillman Hunter with Kangaroo, blue, decals applied, lacks front bumper but does include the leaflet and kangaroo figure. Good in good plus box with inner pictorial display stand. Sold for £90, Vectis, March.

Corgi Toys No 334 Mini Cooper "Magnifique", metallic blue, with off-white interior and red/yellow striped sliding sunroof. Excellent in fair window box. Sold for £50, Vectis, March.

Tri-ang Spot-on No 260 Royal Rolls-Royce, maroon, with Queen & Duke of Edinburgh figures, 2 figures to front of car. Good on grey plastic base with clear perspex top. Sold for £70, Vectis, March.

Corgi Toys No 270 "James Bond" Aston Martin DB5, silver, red interior with James Bond figure only, fitted with Whizzwheels (2nd issue), plus gold front and rear bumpers. Good plus in good striped window box. Sold for £70, Vectis, March.

Tri-ang Spot-On 157/SL Rover 3 litre, pale turquoise, cream interior with black steering wheel and driver figure, chrome trim, cast spun hubs. Excellent plus in fair carded picture box with correct battery-operated instruction leaflet. Sold for £140, Vectis, March.

Corgi Toys No 245 Buick Riviera, metallic blue with red interior, light wear to the bright plated bumpers. Excellent in good plus card box. Sold for £60, Vectis, March.

Tri-ang Spot-On No 113 Aston Martin DB Mk3, pale blue, off white interior, spoked wheels and silver trim. Good plus to excellent in good box. Sold for £160, Vectis, March.

Benbros Mighty Midget & TV Series No 40 Ford Convertible, light blue with silver detailing and larger treaded unpainted cast wheels. Excellent to near mint in good plus to excellent Mighty Midget box. Sold for £45, Vectis, March.

Benbros Mighty Midget & TV Series No 49 Coca-Cola Truck, yellow with silver detailing and "DRINK Coca-Cola" on both sides of central header and rear tail boards, with larger black plastic treaded wheels. Good plus to excellent in good plus to excellent Mighty Midget box. Sold for £80, Vectis, March.

Matchbox Models of Yesteryear Y3 1910 Benz Limousine, cream body and chassis, Chartreuse yellow roof, dark red seats and grille, cream metal steering wheel, brass 12-spoke wheels, cast rear wing infill web, 2 holes to baseplate. Excellent plus, unboxed. Sold for £150, Vectis, March.

Matchbox Models of Yesteryear Y3 1910 Benz Limousine, dark metallic green body and chassis, Chartreuse yellow roof, dark red seats and grille, black plastic steering wheels, brass 12-spoke wheels, without holes to baseplate. Near mint, unboxed. Sold for £320, Vectis, March.

Matchbox Models of Yesteryear Y6 1913 Cadillac, pre-production colour trial model - light grey body without side cutouts, blue chassis, red seats and grille, unplated windscreen without lug, smooth tan roof without locating pips and type A baseplate. Excellent, unboxed. Sold for £560, Vectis, March.

Matchbox Models of Yesteryear Y10 1908 Grand Prix Mercedes, white body, black chassis, dark green seat, plated parts, thin rear brace, crimped axles. Excellent, unboxed. Sold for £80, Vectis, March.

Matchbox Models of Yesteryear Y10 1906 Rolls-Royce Silver Ghost, pre-production colour trial model - blue body and chassis, bright red seats, dark red grille, unplated parts and wheels. Excellent, unboxed. Sold for £850, Vectis, March.

Matchbox Models of Yesteryear Y13 1862 American "General" Class Locomotive - "Santa Fe", light green body, dark red chassis, black base, dark red baseplate rivet, gold condenser tops, silver headlamp lens, gold boiler door, type A piston slot, light green valve and Lesney England base. Excellent plus, unboxed. Sold for £280, Vectis, March.

Matchbox Models of Yesteryear Y16 1904 Spyker Veteran Automobile, maroon body and chassis, maroon radiator shell, brass 12-spoke wheels with wheel rim bolt head detail, black knobbly tyres, type 1 chassis to running board panel and baseplate type A with single rear ejector ring cast beneath axles. Good plus to excellent, unboxed. Sold for £5800, Vectis, March.

Matchbox Models of Yesteryear Y24 1928 Bugatti T44, colour trial model - plum red body with black door panels, brown seats, gold plated parts with black grille, cream chassis, chrome 24-spoke wheels, black rear luggage trunk, 13mm rear window with type 2 closed rear mudguard gaps. Near mint, unboxed. Sold for £140, Vectis, March.

Matchbox Dinky CON-08 Code 2 Dinner Model "25th MICA UK Convention" Harrogate 2010, metallic silver body, metallic blue base and wheelarches, multi-coloured logos with "Malcolm Saunders" to roof - one of only 35 issued. Excellent. Sold for £60, Vectis, March.

Matchbox Models of Yesteryear Y16 1928 Mercedes Benz SS Coupe, silver body, metallic red chassis, black seats and grille, black textured hood, black smooth rear luggage trunk, brass 24-spoke wheels, separate brass exhaust and with cast rear axle differential. Near mint in good type G window box. Sold for £90, Vectis, March.

Matchbox Models of Yesteryear Y24 1928 Bugatti T44, late colour trail model - burnt orange body, glossy black chassis, beige seats, matt silver plated parts, chrome 24-spoke wheels with screwed baseplate not riveted. Near mint in type I straw window box. Sold for £60, Vectis, March.

Matchbox Superfast Peterbilt Tanker - "Avia", red/white with grey plastic aerial, chrome parts and wheels on Belgium export blister card. Mint on excellent card. Sold for £60, Vectis, March.

Matchbox Regular Wheels 44a Rolls-Royce Silver Cloud, metallic light blue, silver trim, knobbly silver plastic wheels with rounded axles. Excellent plus in good picture box. Sold for £40, Vectis, March.

Britains 9529 Massey Ferguson 135 Tractor, red, white, grey with driver figure and separate accessories. Excellent plus, excellent inner carded tray, good outer carded box. Sold for £200, Vectis, March.

CIJ (France) 3/5 Dyna Junior, pale green, cream detachable hood, dark red seat and straps, black windscreen, silver trim, spun hubs and white tyres. Excellent in good carded picture box. Sold for £80, Vectis, March.

Dinky (Nicky Toys) 142 Jaguar Mark X, silver, pale grey interior.- Excellent in fair carded picture box. Sold for £70, Vectis, March.

Corgi Toys "Chitty Chitty Bang Bang", recent limited edition production replica, includes 4 figures with opening stabilisers and spare rear stabiliser for separate attachment. Near mint, including leaflet, certificate and instruction slip, in excellent card box with inner packaging. Sold for £60, Vectis, March.

Corgi Toys No 270 "James Bond" Aston Martin DB5, silver, red interior with James Bond figure only, and tyre slashers. Good plus in fair to good 1st issue wing flap presentation bubble pack (missing inner card and instruction pack). Sold for £120, Vectis, March.

Corgi pair of "James Bond's" Aston Martin DB5 - Goldfinger 50th Anniversary, 1x silver No 04203 silver, 1x No 04204 gold. Mint in near mint specially produced 'action' packaging. Sold for £70, Vectis, March.

Corgi No 96655 "James Bond" Aston Martin DB5, silver, red interior and tyre slashers, 1995 reissue model. Mint in excellent plus striped window box. Sold for £45, Vectis, March.

Corgi Toys 150S Vanwall Formula 1 Grand Prix Racing Car, red, with suspension, driver, blue/white bonnet racing no 25, flat spun wheels with spoked decals applied, in near mint original condition, with an excellent original blue/yellow box. Sold for £95, C&T Auctioneers, May.

Corgi Toys 151 Lotus Mark Eleven Le Mans Racing Car, blue body, red seats, clear windscreen, racing no '3' in mint original condition, with an excellent original blue/yellow box, 3/6 in pencil to one end flap. Sold for £95, C&T Auctioneers, May.

Corgi Toys 152 B.R.M, Formula 1 Grand Prix Racing Car, dark green body, yellow seat, racing number '17' flat spun wheels in mint original condition, with a good original blue picture box, some slight age wear, Corgi model club leaflet. Sold for £70, C&T Auctioneers, May.

Corgi Toys 155 Roger Clarkes Lotus Climax Formula 1 Racing Car, green body, driver no '1' spun wheels, in mint original condition, inner card packing, with an excellent original box, 5/3 in pencil to one end flap. Sold for £50, C&T Auctioneers, May.

Corgi Toys 200 Ford Consul Saloon, two tone cream/ bright green body, flat spun wheel hubs, in excellent original bright condition, some slight paint rubbing to high lines on casting with a fair to good original blue/yellow picture box, with edge/age wear. Sold for £110, C&T Auctioneers, May.

Corgi Toys 211 Studebaker "Golden Hawk", blue body, gold rear wing flashes, flat spun wheels, in excellent to near mint original condition, a couple of tiny paint chips, original early blue box is near mint, 3/9 in pencil to one end flap, with Corgi club leaflet. Sold for £95, C&T Auctioneers, May.

Corgi Toys 233 Heinkel Economy Car, orange body, silver trim, yellow interior, cast spun wheels, in mint original condition, with a mint blue and yellow original illustrated box, Corgi model club TV21 leaflet. Sold for £85, C&T Auctioneers, May.

Corgi Toys 256 Volkswagen 1200 in East African Safari Trim, orange body, brown interior, right hand drive, spun wheel hubs, with original grey Rhinoceros, in near mint original condition, inner card illustrated stand is excellent, outer card box is good, complete with all end flaps, some age/edge wear Sold for £140, C&T Auctioneers, May.

A boxed Corgi Army fuel Tanker, #1134. Sold for £140, Stacey's Auctioneers, June.

A boxed Dinky Supertoys Leyland Octopus Wagon, #934. Sold for £40, Stacey's Auctioneers, June.

A Dinky Coventry Climax Fork Lift Truck, boxed. Sold for £25, Stacey's Auctioneers, June.

A Dinky Supertoys Foden 14-Ton Tanker boxed, appears to be re-painted. Sold for £25, Stacey's Auctioneers, June.

A Dinky Toys boxed Pullmore Car Transporter, boxed, #982 with loading ramp. Sold for £30, Stacey's Auctioneers, June.

A Dinky Blaw Knox Bulldozer, boxed #561. Sold for £20, Stacey's Auctioneers, June.

A Corgi Simon Snorkel Fire Engine, boxed #1127. Sold for £40, Stacey's Auctioneers, June.

A Corgi Toys Bedford Van "Daily Express", boxed #403. Sold for £50, Stacey's Auctioneers, June.

A Dinky Supertoys Elevator Loader, boxed #964. Sold for £25, Stacey's Auctioneers, June.

A Corgi Toys Whizzwheels Adams Bros, Probe 16, boxed, #384. Sold for £18, Stacey's Auctioneers, June.

A Corgi Gift set 4 Country Farm set, boxed, #GS4. Sold for £85, Stacey's Auctioneers, June.

A Corgi Bedford Horse Transporter, boxed, #1104. Sold for £45, Stacey's Auctioneers, June.

A Corgi Horse Transporter, boxed, #1105. Sold for £35, Stacey's Auctioneers, June.

A Boxed Corgi Unimog Tipper, #409. Sold for £20, Stacey's Auctioneers, June.

A Corgi Mini Marcos GT 850, boxed, #341. Sold for £40, Stacey's Auctioneers, June.

A corgi Mini Marcos GT850, boxed, #341. Sold for £35, Stacey's Auctioneers, June.

A Corgi Ghia 5000 Mangusta, with De Tomaso Chassis, boxed, #271. Sold for £70, Stacey's Auctioneers, June.

A Corgi Lotus-Climax Formula 1 Racing Car, boxed, #155. Sold for £45, Stacey's Auctioneers, June.

A Boxed Corgi Ghia L.6.4, #242. Sold for £25, Stacey's Auctioneers, June.

A Corgi Bentley Series 'T', , boxed, #274. Sold for £30, Stacey's Auctioneers, June.

A Corgi Proteus-Cambell "Bluebird" Record Car, boxed, #153. Sold for £50, Stacey's Auctioneers, June.

A Lotus Racing Team Gift Set, boxed, #37. Sold for £200, Stacey's Auctioneers, June.

A Corgi Massey-Ferguson 165 Tractor, boxed, #66. Sold for £40, Stacey's Auctioneers, June.

A Corgi Chrysler "Imperial", boxed, #246. Sold for £35, Stacey's Auctioneers, June.

Matchbox Lesney Superfast G-3 Racing Specials Set, metallic blue 5e Lotus Europa, metallic red 20d Lamborghini Marzal, metallic green 45c Ford Group 6, metallic purple 52c Dodge Charger, metallic gold 56c BMC 1800 Pinifarina and metallic red 68c Porsche 910 - some decals missing. Good to very good in fair to good outer window box, with excellent white inner tray, but missing original outer shrink wrap. Sold for £120, C&T Auctioneers, June.

Matchbox Lesney G-2 "Big Mover" Set, yellow/orange K-11 DAF Car Transporter, metallic green 9 AMX Javelin, metallic crimson 32 Maserati Bora, metallic blue 4 Pontiac Firebird, yellow/black 44 Boss Mustang and metallic red 51 Citroën SM. Mint in very good outer window box with good inner plastic tray. Sold for £120, C&T Auctioneers, June.

Team Matchbox Superfast Champions Set, K7 racing car transporter, 2x 24d Team Matchbox racing cars (1x metallic green, 1x metallic red), 2x 34d F1 racing cars (1x metallic blue, 1x orange), missing Team Surtees car sticker and badge. Excellent to near mint in good box (fair amount of felt pen graffiti), but missing shrink wrap. Sold for £110, C&T Auctioneers, June.

Matchbox Adventure 2000 K-2002 Flight Hunter pre-production, yellow body, black base, chrome interior, amber glass. Fair to good, unboxed. Sold for £160, C&T Auctioneers, June.

Matchbox Superfast 900 Twin Pack TP-32, orange 1g 'Revin Rebel' Dodge Challenger with blue roof, yellow 74c Toe Joe "Hitch Hiker" with red arms. Mint in very good punched blister pack. Sold for £95, C&T Auctioneers, June.

Matchbox Superfast Military Strike Force Gift Set 11, 16 Badger Radar Truck, TP-16 Military Case Tractor, 38 Jeep, 73 Rolamatics Weasel Armoured Car, TP-15 Mercedes Truck & Trailer. Mint in excellent outer window box with excellent inner plastic tray. Sold for £75, C&T Auctioneers, June.

Matchbox Superfast Railway G-2 Set, ready to assemble station, plastic track, 43 0-4-0 loco, 2x 44 passenger coaches, flat car and flat car with container. Mint in mint box. Sold for £90, C&T Auctioneers, June.

Dinky Toys No 27AK Farm Tractor and Hay Rake, red Massey Harris tractor and hay rake with yellow wheels. Excellent in good box with inner base packing. Sold for £85, C&T Auctioneers, June.

Dinky Toys No 982 Pullmore Car transporter and No 794 Loading Ramp, mid-blue cab and hubs, light blue back. Excellent in very good box with packing piece and very good loading ramp box. Sold for £60, C&T Auctioneers, June.

Matchbox Speedkings K-57 Javelin "Drag Race" Pack, red Javelin with green "Milligan's Mill" on yellow trailer. Near mint in good box. Sold for £110, C&T Auctioneers, June.

Matchbox Speedkings K-58 Corvette "Power Boat" Pack, blue "Caper Cart" with orange and white "Chrysler" speedboat on yellow trailer. Near mint in very good box. Sold for £85, C&T Auctioneers, June.

Sun Star No 2912 1/24 scale Routemaster RMC London Transport Bus, Green Line livery on route 715 to Guildford. Mint in excellent to near mint box. Sold for £140, C&T Auctioneers, June.

Sun Star No 2923 1/24 scale "The RT series" 1947 RT402, London Transport livery on route 10 to Abridge, Genasprin and John Bull adverts. Mint in excellent to near mint box. Sold for £540, C&T Auctioneers, June.

Sun Star No 2920 1/24 scale "The RT series" 1939 RT113, London Transport livery on route 37 to Peckham, National War Bonds and Picture Post adverts. Mint in excellent to near mint box. Sold for £120, C&T Auctioneers, June.

Dinky Toys No 60 British Aeroplane Set, second issue example comprising No 60a Imperial Airways Liner, No 60b D.H. Leopard Moth, No 60c Percival Gull, No 60d Low Wing Monoplane, No 60e General Monospar plus No 60f Cierva Autogiro. Very good to mint in very good pale blue box. Sold for £900, Wallis & Wallis, June.

Dinky Toys No 60 Aeroplane Set, second issue comprising No 60a Imperial Airways Liner, No 60b D.H. Leopard Moth, No 60c Percival Gull, No 60d Low Wing Monoplane, No 60e General Monospar plus No 60f Cierva Autogiro. Good to mint in very good box. Sold for £850, Wallis & Wallis, June.

Dinky Toys No 66 Camouflaged Aeroplane Set, war-time issue, comprising No 66a Heavy Bomber, No 66b Dive Bomber Fighter, No 66c Two Seater Fighter, No 66d Dive Bomber, No 66e Medium Bomber, all in camouflage livery, plus a silver No 66f Cierva Autogiro. Very good in very good box. Sold for £1200, Wallis & Wallis, June.

Dinky Toys No 65 Aeroplane Set, comprising No 60c Douglas DC3, No 60r Empire Flying Boat, No 60v Armstrong Whitworth 'Whitley' Bomber, No 60w Clipper III Flying Boat, No 62n Junkers JU90, No 62p Armstrong Whitworth 'Ensign', No 62r de Havilland 'Albatross' Mail Liner and No 62w Imperial Airways 'Frobisher' Class Airliner. Mint in very good box. Sold for £1800, Wallis & Wallis, June.

French Dinky No 883 Military Char AMX Poseur De Pont, in drab military green. Very good in very good box, with instruction leaflet. Sold for £70, Wallis & Wallis, June.

Matchbox Superfast No 14a Iso Grifo, metallic dark blue body, clear windows, dark blue interior, bare metal base, solid 5-spoke narrow wheels with tread pattern cast. Near mint in excellent plus type F2 transitional box. Sold for £170, Vectis, June.

Matchbox Superfast No 15a Volkswagen Beetle, off-white body with racing number 137 door labels and Monte Carlo Rally front bumper decal, ivory interior, bare metal base with single rear bumper, solid 5-spoke narrow wheels with tread pattern cast. Near mint in good plus type F1 transitional box. Sold for £130, Vectis, June.

Matchbox Superfast No 27a Mercedes 230 SL, off-white body, red interior, bare metal base, solid small diameter 5-spoke narrow wheels. Excellent plus in near mint to mint type F3 transitional box. Sold for £80, Vectis, June.

Matchbox Superfast No 36a Opel Diplomat, metallic light gold body with silver grille, chrome engine, clear windows, white interior, gloss black base, hollow small diameter 5-spoke narrow wheels. Mint in excellent to excellent plus type F3 box. Sold for £60, Vectis, June.

Matchbox Superfast No 46a Mercedes 300 SE Coupe, metallic blue body with opening doors, clear windows, ivory interior, bare metal base, hollow 5-spoke narrow wheels without tread pattern cast. Near mint in excellent plus type F3 transitional box. Sold for £380, Vectis, June.

Matchbox Superfast No 46a Mercedes 300 SE Coupe, metallic gold body with opening doors, clear windows, ivory interior, bare metal base, solid 5-spoke narrow wheels with tread pattern cast.- Excellent in excellent type F3 transitional box. Sold for £100, Vectis, June.

Matchbox Superfast No 67a Volkswagen 1600 TL, red body, clear windows, ivory interior, bare metal base, solid 5-spoke narrow wheels with tread pattern cast. Near mint to mint in excellent type F2 transitional box. Sold for £100, Vectis, June.

Matchbox Superfast No 8a Ford Mustang, white body, clear windows, red interior, gloss black base, 5-spoke wide wheels. Excellent to excellent plus in good plus type G box. Sold for £240, Vectis, June.

Matchbox Superfast No 8a Ford Mustang, burnt orange body, clear windows, ivory interior, gloss black base, 5-spoke wide wheels. Excellent plus in good plus to excellent type G box. Sold for £170, Vectis, June.

Matchbox Superfast No 22a Pontiac GP Coupe, metallic dark purple body without silver trim, clear windows, grey interior, gloss black base, hollow small diameter 5-spoke narrow wheels. Excellent plus in excellent type G box. Sold for £220, Vectis, June.

Matchbox Superfast No 29a American La France Fire Pumper Truck, bare metal base, solid small diameter 5-spoke narrow wheels with black axle clips. Near mint in good type G box. Sold for £120, Vectis, June.

Matchbox Superfast No 44a GMC Refrigerator Truck, red cab & chassis, turquoise green body, dark green windows, 4-spoke narrow wheels with black axle clips. Excellent in excellent plus to near mint type G box. Sold for £260, Vectis, June.

Matchbox Superfast No 53a Ford Zodiac, lime green body, clear windows, ivory interior, bare metal base, 5-spoke wide wheels. Near mint in excellent type G box. Sold for £120, Vectis, June.

Matchbox Superfast No c.1970 issue 48-Car Carry Case, containing a selection of 48 mostly early to mid-1970s issue models. Excellent to mint in good plus carry case. Sold for £320, Vectis, June.

Matchbox Regular Wheels No 68b Mercedes Coach, factory colour trial - primrose yellow body & base with closed axles, white plastic roof, clear windows, white interior with low seats, 36-tread black plastic wheels with factory spun axle ends. Good to good plus, unboxed. Sold for £620, Vectis, June.

Matchbox Regular Wheels No 34b Volkswagen Transporter Caravette Camper, factory colour trial - blue body with bare metal opening doors, turquoise green windows, green interior & riveted base, 45-tread black plastic wheels with un-spun axle ends. Excellent plus, unboxed. Sold for £440, Vectis, June.

Matchbox Regular Wheels No 56b Jaguar 3.8 Saloon, factory colour trial - green body and opening bonnet without silver trim, 36-tread black plastic wheel with unspun axle ends, turquoise green glazing unit. Good plus, unboxed. Sold for £1200, Vectis, June.

French Dinky Toys No 808 Camion G.M.C. Militaire Depannage, drab military green. Very good in excellent box with insert. Sold for £80, Wallis & Wallis, June.

French Dinky Toys No 815 Sinpar 4x4 Gendarmerie Militaire, Renault 4 in olive green, with 2 Police figures, plastic tilt, aerial and radio, with unused decal sheet. Mint in very good box. Sold for £90, Wallis & Wallis, June.

French Dinky Toys No 24B Berline 403 Peugeot, light grey, plated ridged wheels with white tyres. Very good to excellent in very good box. Sold for £55, Wallis & Wallis, June

French Dinky Toys No 24F Familiale 403 Peugeot, light blue, plated ridged wheels with white tyres, period French number plates and 'F' decal to front and rear. Very good to excellent in very good box. Sold for £55, Wallis & Wallis, June.

Dinky Toys No 101 Sunbeam Alpine Sports, cerise with cream interior, cream wheels and black tyres, with driver. Very good to excellent in very good box. Sold for £90, Wallis & Wallis, June.

Dinky Supertoys No 60F/891 Caravelle S.E. 210 Airliner, white, silver and blue Air France livery, F-BGNY registration to wings. Very good in very good box. Sold for £80, Wallis & Wallis, June.

Dinky Toys No 63 Mayo Composite Aircraft, both in silver with red propellers, with registrations G-ADHJ and G-ADHK. Very good in very good box. Sold for £260, Wallis & Wallis, June.

Dinky Supertoys No 919 Guy Van Golden Shred, red, with yellow wheels and black tyres. Very good to excellent in excellent box. Sold for £280, Wallis & Wallis, June.

Dinky Supertoys No 930 Bedford Pallet Jekta Van, yellow and orange, yellow wheels with black tyres and 3x pallets. Mint in good box, with instruction leaflet. Sold for £240, Wallis & Wallis, June.

Dinky Toys No 31 Holland Coachcraft Van, red with gold painted trim line and off-white lettering, plated wheels with white rubber tyres. Fair to good condition, with one windscreen pillar broken and fatigue to roof front. Sold for £180, Wallis & Wallis, June.

Dinky Supertoys No 514 Guy Van Weetabix, yellow, with yellow wheels, black tyres. Mint in very good box. Sold for £2100, Wallis & Wallis, June.

Dinky Toys No 297 Police Vehicles Gift Set, comprising long-wheelbase Ford Transit in white and orange 'Accident Unit' livery, Austin Cooper 'S' Mini and a Ford Zodiac, both in white, 'POLICE SLOW' and 'POLICE ACCIDENT' signs and 4 cones. Very good to mint in very good box with near mint inner display plinth and 2x packing pieces. Sold for £260, Wallis & Wallis, June.

Dinky Toys No 246 International GT Gift Set, comprising 3 sports cars - De Tomaso Mangusta 5000 in white and fluorescent pink with black interior, Ford G.T. Racing Car in metallic green, RN7 with red interior, and Dino Ferrari in metallic blue with black engine cover, RN20, yellow interior. Mint with near mint outer box and insert. Sold for £220, Wallis & Wallis, June.

Dinky Toys shop and cinema card display for the Battle of Britain film, fold together cardboard display complete with both aircraft - No 719 Spitfire MkII and No 721 Junkers Ju 87B Stuka, complete with bomb. Excellent on excellent to near mint display unit. Sold for £360, Wallis & Wallis, June.

Dinky Toys Gift Set No 4 Racing Cars, comprising 5 single seat racing cars - dark green No 233 Cooper-Bristol with RN6, red No 232 Alfa Romeo with RN8, dark blue/yellow No 234 Ferrari with RN5, light green No 235 H.W.M. with RN7, and red No 231 Maserati (231) with RN9. Very good to mint in fair to good box. Sold for £480, Wallis & Wallis, June.

Corgi Toys Gift Set GS3 Batmobile & Batboat, with Whizzwheels, light blue glazing, both figures in car, none in boat, gold-painted trailer, most rockets on plastic sprue. Very good in very good box. Sold for £300, Wallis & Wallis, June.

Corgi Toys Gift Set 32 Lotus Elite and JPS Racing Car on Transporter, in black and gold JPS livery, complete with trailer. Very good to mint in excellent box. Sold for £45, Wallis & Wallis, June.

Corgi Toys No 1121 Chipperfields Circus Crane Truck, red with blue detailing, bare metal jib and yellow crane mount. Very good plus in good box. Sold for £40, Sheffield Auction Gallery, July.

Corgi Toys No 1127 Simon Snorkel Fire Engine, red with figures present. Very good plus in very good picture box. Sold for £30, Sheffield Auction Gallery, July.

Corgi Toys No 483 Dodge Kew Fargo Tipper, white cab with blue back. Excellent, in excellent box. Sold for £35, Sheffield Auction Gallery, July.

Corgi Toys No 318 Lotus Elan S2, blue, rear transfer in tact - extra racing number added to boot area. Very good in excellent box. Sold for £28, Sheffield Auction Gallery, July.

Corgi Toys No 229 Chevrolet Corvair, mid-blue. Very good plus in very good box. Sold for £25, Sheffield Auction Gallery, July.

Corgi Toys No 438 Land Rover, green body with grey plastic canopy. Very good plus in very good box. Sold for £40, Sheffield Auction Gallery, July.

Dinky Toys No 954 Vega Major Luxury Coach, white with maroon and silver trim and blue interior, non-electric. Very good plus, in very good box. Sold for £40, Sheffield Auction Gallery, July.

Dinky No 974 AEC Hoyner Car Transporter, red cab and chassis with orange (lower) and yellow (upper) trailer. Excellent in very good box with instructions and wheel ramps still in packet. Sold for £65, Sheffield Auction Gallery, July.

Dinky Toys No 451 Johnston Road Sweeper, orange cab with metallic green rear body. Excellent in excellent box with inserts. Sold for £25, Sheffield Auction Gallery, July.

Dinky Toys No 255 Mersey Tunnel Police Van, red with yellow lettering. Very good plus in very good box. Sold for £45, Sheffield Auction Gallery, July.

Dinky Toys No 142 Jaguar Mark X, blue, with luggage. Excellent in excellent box. Sold for £45, Sheffield Auction Gallery, July.

Dinky Toys No 109 Gabriel Model 'T' Ford, from The Secret Service TV show. Excellent in excellent box with all correct inserts. Sold for £35, Sheffield Auction Gallery, July.

Dinky Toys No 300 Massey Harris Tractor, red with yellow wheels and dull yellow driver figure. Very good plus in good plus box. Sold for £35, Sheffield Auction Gallery, July.

Dinky Toys No 188 Jensen FF, yellow. Excellent in good original plastic case. Sold for £35, Sheffield Auction Gallery, July.

Dinky Toys No 131 Jaguar E-Type 2+2, bronze. Very good plus in good original plastic case. Sold for £30, Sheffield Auction Gallery, July.

Dinky Toys No 190 Monteverdi 375L, dark metallic red with Speedwheels. Very good in good original plastic case. Sold for £30, Sheffield Auction Gallery, July.

Dinky Toys No 344 Land Rover, in metallic blue with Speedwheels, silver rear body interior and engine bay, red cab interior. Excellent in excellent box. Sold for £40, Sheffield Auction Gallery, July.

Dinky Toys No 165 Ford Capri, metallic green. Excellent, with mint plastic bubble and excellent card plinth. Sold for £40, Sheffield Auction Gallery, July.

Corgi Toys early original free-standing wooden shop display case, 2x wooden flaps to rear for support, inner is finished in white with pale blue wooden shelves and "Corgi Toys" signage, missing glass front. Good, approximately 48" x 32". Sold for £520, Vectis, July.

Tri-ang Spot-on No 274 Morris 1100, pale blue, red interior, chrome front and rear bumpers, cast spun hubs, grey plastic roof rack with red and blue canoe. Good to good plus, inner carded tray is good plus, outer window box is poor. Sold for £70, Vectis, July.

Corgi Toys No 311 Ford Capri V6 3-litre, fluorescent body, black interior, red-spot wheels. Excellent plus in near mint window box. Sold for £220, Vectis, July.

Corgi Toys No 374 Jaguar E-Type, pearlescent yellow body, brown interior, black base, chrome trim, Whizzwheels. Near mint in good plus window box. Sold for £50, Vectis, July.

Corgi Toys No 202 Renault 16TS, blue body, yellow interior, chrome trim and base, grey plastic tow hook, Whizzwheels. Excellent plus in excellent plus window box. Sold for £60, Vectis, July.

Corgi Toys No 317 Jaguar E-Type Competition Model, chrome-plated finish, black interior with driver figure, blue, white and black racing number 2 decal, wire wheels with black treaded tyres. Good to good plus in good box with collectors club folded leaflet. Sold for £80, Vectis, July.

Corgi Toys No 223 Chevrolet State Patrol Car, black body, lemon interior, grey plastic aerial, silver trim and side flashes, flat spun hubs with accessory packs applied. Excellent plus in good plus box with correct inner packing piece. Sold for £50, Vectis, July.

Corgi Toys No 210S Citroën DS19, red body, grey base, lemon interior, silver trim, spun hubs. Excellent plus in good plus to excellent blue and yellow carded picture box. Sold for £120, Vectis, July.

Corgi Toys No 302 Hillman Hunter with Kangaroo, blue body, white roof, black bonnet, kangaroo, instructions, partially used transfers. Excellent in good plus box, inner stand excellent. Sold for £110, Warwick & Warwick, July.

Corgi Toys Gift Set No 24 Commer Constructor Set, 2 cab/chassis units, 4 interchangeable bodies, milkman figure, milk crates and bench seat insert. Excellent in excellent box with excellent polystyrene tray, with instructions. Sold for £70, Warwick & Warwick, July.

Corgi Toys Gift Set No 33 Fordson "Power Major" Tractor with Beast Carrier and Animals, Fordson Power Major Tractor (blue body, orange plastic hubs, silver seat - No 55) and Beast Carrier (yellow trailer, red hubs and chassis - No 58), 4 calves. Excellent in fair box, good plus inner stand. Sold for £75, Warwick & Warwick, July.

Dinky Toys No 103 Captain Scarlet Spectrum Patrol Car, metallic red body, white base, blue tinted windows, yellow interior. Excellent in good plus box, without inner stand. Sold for £220, Warwick & Warwick, July.

Dinky Toys No 104 Captain Scarlet Spectrum Pursuit Vehicle, blue body and base, white front bumper, 2 rockets, and Captain Scarlet figure. Excellent in good box with good inner stand, 1 packing piece and instructions. Sold for £180, Warwick & Warwick, July.

Dinky Toys No 105 Captain Scarlet Maximum Security Vehicle, white body, red base and side stripes, red interior, 'radioactive' crate. Excellent in good plus box. Sold for £110, Warwick & Warwick, July.

Dinky Toys No 301 Field Marshall Tractor, orange body, silver wheels, tan driver. Excellent in good dual-numbered box (27N/301). Sold for £140, Warwick & Warwick, July.

Dinky Toys No 501 Foden Diesel 8-Wheel Wagon, 1st type cab, grey cab and back, red flash and hubs, black chassis. Good plus in nearly good box with red and white label. Sold for £180, Warwick & Warwick, July.

Dinky Toys No 118 Tow Away Glider Set, blue/white Triumph 2000, red/cream trailer, red/yellow glider. Excellent in good pictorial box, excellent inner stand with 1 packing piece and instructions. Sold for £180, Warwick & Warwick, July.

Matchbox Superfast No 1b Mod Rod, lemon yellow body with Spotted Cat hood label, dark amber windows, rare red interior, bare metal base. Near mint in excellent "New" type H box. Sold for £50, Vectis, July.

Matchbox Superfast No 1d Dodge Challenger, orange body without tampo print, blue roof, clear windows, black interior, silver painted base. Near mint to mint in excellent plus type L box. Sold for £240, Vectis, July.

Matchbox Superfast No 4b Gruesome Twosome, metallic orange-gold body, rare dark amber windows, lemon yellow interior, bare metal base, 5-spoke wheels. Excellent in excellent "New" type H box. Sold for £850, Vectis, July.

Matchbox Superfast No 4d '57 Chevy, metallic pale pink body & hood, clear windows, chrome interior, bare metal base, rare dot-dash front wheels, 5-crown rear wheels. Excellent plus in excellent plus type L box. Sold for £800, Vectis, July.

Matchbox Superfast No 5a Lotus Europa, black body with gold "JPS" tampo print, clear windows, ivory interior, bare metal base with cast shut tow slot, 5-spoke wide wheels. Excellent in fair complete rare Japanese Issue "New" model No 18 type I box. Sold for £150, Vectis, July.

Matchbox Superfast No 6c Mercedes 350SL Convertible, metallic silver body with silver side stripes, clear windscreen, white interior, silver painted base, rare Maltese Cross wheels. Mint in excellent scarce type L box. Sold for £170, Vectis, July.

Matchbox Superfast No 7c Volkswagen Golf, metallic silver body with green tampo printed side stripes, clear windows, red interior, matt black base. Near mint in excellent scarce late issue type L box. Sold for £130, Vectis, July.

Matchbox Superfast No 8a Ford Mustang, white body, clear windows, red interior, gloss black base, 5-spoke wide wheels. Excellent plus in mint type F3 transitional box. Sold for £380, Vectis, July.

Matchbox Superfast No 8b Ford Mustang Wildcat Dragster, orange body with type 2 labels, dark green windows, dark yellow interior, gloss black base, 5-spoke front & rear wheels. Excellent in mint type G box. Sold for £180, Vectis, July.

Matchbox Superfast No 12b Setra Coach, lemon yellow body with thin rear bumper casting, white roof, turquoise green windows, ivory interior, hollow 5-spoke narrow wheels. Excellent plus in mint "New" type G box. Sold for £120, Vectis, July.

Matchbox Superfast No 12c Big Bull Bulldozer, orange body, chrome interior, metallic green chassis & blade, rare black plastic rollers, original & pliable black rubber tracks. Near mint to mint "New" type I box. Sold for £120, Vectis, July.

Matchbox Superfast No 12d Citroën CX Estate, metallic blue body, clear windows, pale yellow interior, rare bare metal base (base has been factory sprayed upside down), dot-dash wheels. Excellent in excellent plus "New" type L box. Sold for £110, Vectis, July.

Matchbox Superfast No 13a Dodge BP Wreck Truck, small diameter 5-spoke wide wheels with black axle clips. Excellent in excellent "New" type G box. Sold for £110, Vectis, July.

Matchbox Superfast No 14a Iso Grifo, blue body with early nose emblem, clear windows, white interior, rare silver painted base, 5-spoke wide wheels. Excellent in mint "New" type H box. Sold for £420, Vectis, July.

Matchbox Superfast No 22a Pontiac GP Coupe, metallic dark purple body without silver trim, clear windows, grey interior, gloss black base, hollow large diameter 5-spoke narrow wheels without tread pattern cast. Excellent in good plus "New" type G box. Sold for £140, Vectis, July.

Matchbox Superfast No 22b Freeman Inter-City Commuter, metallic purple body without labels, clear windows, ivory interior, bare metal base, 5-spoke wheels. Excellent plus in near mint "New" type G box. Sold for £120, Vectis, July.

Matchbox Superfast No 24b Team Matchbox Racing Car, lemon yellow body with blue background racing number 4 nose label, bare metal base, Maltese Cross wheels. Near mint in near mint "New" type I box. Sold for £260, Vectis, July.

Matchbox Superfast No 29a American La France Fire Pumper Truck, red body, blue windows & roof light, bare metal base, solid small diameter 5-spoke narrow wheels with black axle clips. Near mint in excellent plus "New" type G box. Sold for £260, Vectis, July.

Matchbox Superfast No 30a Faun Crane Truck, red cab & chassis, rare orange crane jib with yellow plastic hook, solid 5-spoke narrow wheels. Excellent in good plus "New" type G box. Sold for £170, Vectis, July.

Matchbox Superfast No 45b BMW 3.0 CSL, red body without hood label, dark green windows with roof light support, pale yellow interior, bare metal base, 5-arch wheels. Excellent in good plus type J box. Sold for £1000, Vectis, July.

Dinky Toys No 447 Parsley's Car Bull Nose Morris, green, black and yellow with swivel-headed Parsley figure. Excellent with fair plus inner stand in good outer box. Sold for £35, British Toy Auctions, August.

Matchbox G1 Commercial Motor Gift Set, very good to excellent in fair plus to good box with inner tray. Sold for £170, British Toy Auctions, August.

Matchbox No 14 Bedford Lomas Ambulance, off-white body, red cross and LCC ambulance decals, smooth roof, white interior and black plastic wheels. Mint in excellent E4 box. Sold for £30, British Toy Auctions, August.

Matchbox Regular Wheels No 11 ERF "Esso" Petrol Tanker, red body, large "Esso" decal to rear, brace between cab and tanker, no holes in base, silver grille and headlights, black plastic 18 tread wheels with dome headed axles. Mint in good plus D2 box. Sold for £45, British Toy Auctions, August.

Corgi Juniors Whizzwheels No 3020 Club Racing Gift Set, light blue (unlisted colour) Ford Capri with white base, red Austin Healey Sprite, metallic purple Land Rover Wrecker Truck, steel blue Ford Escort Mk I, maroon Ferrari 512S and metallic purple Mini Cooper, complete with figures and cones in bags. Near mint to mint. Sold for £560, Vectis, August.

Dinky Toys No 299 Post Office Services Gift Set, red Morris Commercial "Royal Mail" Delivery Van, green Morris "Post Office Telephones" Service Van, 2x figures and Public Telephone Box. Near mint to mint. Sold for £300, Vectis, August.

Dinky Toys No 351 "UFO" Shado Interceptor, green, blue tinted windows, chrome interior, red legs, with white and orange missile, comes with No 7 catalogue showing an Interceptor on the front cover and two signed trading cards. Good plus to excellent. Sold for £480, Vectis, August.

Dinky Toys No 353 "UFO" Shado 2 Mobile, green body, off white interior, large brown rollers with grey rubber tracks, with yellow and red missile. Near mint in good plus carded picture box with correct inner packing piece and instruction leaflet. Sold for £300, Vectis, August.

French Dinky No 823 GMC Water Tanker, drab green including concave hubs and Tanker with filler caps, black plastic canopy, with road sign. Near Mint, inner carded tray is near mint, outer carded picture box is good plus to excellent. Sold for £520, Vectis, August.

Corgi Toys No 258 "The Saint's" Car Volvo P1800, white body, blue bonnet label, red interior with figure driver, silver trim, spun hubs. Excellent in good plus blue and yellow carded picture box with collectors club leaflet. Sold for £300, Vectis, August.

Corgi Toys GS37 "Lotus Racing Team" Gift Set, green Lotus Climax Racing Car with racing number 1, yellow Lotus Elan Coupe, green Lotus Elan S2, white Volkswagen Breakdown Van, red trailer with cones in bag, racing numbers 7 and 2 unapplied label sheets plus driver figure. Near mint to mint, polystyrene tray is near mint, outer blue and yellow window box is good plus, with "Mr Retailer" card and instruction/collectors club folded leaflet. Sold for £380, Vectis, August.

Corgi Toys No 270 James Bond Aston Martin DB5, silver, red interior with James Bond and bandit figures, tyre slashers, gold front and rear bumpers. Excellent plus in good slimline blue and yellow window box, with accessory pack (sealed). Sold for £360, Vectis, August.

Corgi Toys GS40 "The Avengers" Gift Set, John Steed's red and black Vintage Bentley with wire wheels and John Steed figure plus 3x original umbrellas, Emma Peel's white Lotus Elan S2 with black interior, spun hubs and Emma Peel figure. Excellent plus to near mint. Sold for £320, Vectis, August.

Corgi Toys No 256 Volkswagen 1200 "East African Safari", orange body, brown interior (left hand drive), racing number 18, spun hubs. Near mint, inner pictorial stand with Rhino figure is excellent in good plus blue and yellow carded picture box with inner packing piece and correct instruction/ collectors club folded leaflet. Sold for £140, Vectis, August.

Corgi Toys No 302 Hillman Hunter "London to Sydney Marathon Winner", blue body, black bonnet, white roof, grey interior, Golden Jacks take-off wheels. Excellent plus, inner pictorial stand is excellent with Kangaroo figure, outer blue and yellow window box is good plus with correct instruction/collectors club folded leaflet. Sold for £120, Vectis, August.

Corgi Toys No 303 Roger Clark's Ford Capri, white body, black bonnet and interior, racing number 73 to doors and bonnet, harder to find variation with red-spot wheels. Excellent plus in excellent orange and yellow window box, with unapplied decal sheet and instruction/collectors club folded leaflet. Sold for £220, Vectis, August.

Corgi Toys No 313 Ford Cortina GXL "Graham Hill", metallic aqua, black roof, off-white interior, black base with Whizzwheels, chrome front and rear bumpers. Near mint in good plus box with Graham Hill figure. Sold for £100, Vectis, August.

Corgi Toys No 313 Ford Cortina GXL "Graham Hill", metallic bronze, black roof, off-white interior, black base with Whizzwheels, chrome front and rear bumpers. Near mint in excellent box. Sold for £120, Vectis, August.

Corgi Toys No 436 Citroën Safari ID19 "Wildlife Preservation", yellow body, brown and green interior with 2x figures, spun hubs, silver trim, with red and green luggage. Excellent in good plus box. Sold for £80, Vectis, August.

Corgi Toys No 475 Citroën Safari "Corgi Ski Club", white body, green and brown interior, silver trim, spun hubs, yellow plastic rack with 4 red skis and sticks. Excellent plus in excellent box. Sold for £110, Vectis, August.

Corgi Toys No 475 Citroën Safari "1964 Olympic Winter Sports", silver trim, spun hubs, yellow rack with 4 red skis, 2 sticks, with figure. Excellent plus in good plus box. Sold for £150, Vectis, August.

Corgi Toys No 492 Volkswagen European Police Car, green, white, brown interior with 2x figures, blue roof light, spun hubs, chrome trim, "Polizei" side decals. Near mint in excellent blue and yellow carded picture box, with inner packing ring and "True Scale Steering" ring. Sold for £110, Vectis, August.

Corgi Toys No 499 Citroën Safari "Grenoble 1968 Winter Olympics", white, blue roof, spun hubs, silver trim, yellow plastic rack with 2x red skis and sticks, with 2 x figures and toboggan. Excellent plus in good to good plus blue and yellow window box, inner carded tray is excellent, with correct instruction/collectors club folded leaflet. Sold for £120, Vectis, August.

Corgi Toys No 513 Citroën Safari "Alpine Rescue", white, red roof and rear hatch, blue interior, grey base, cast hubs, silver trim, yellow plastic rack with 2x skis and sticks with toboggan plus 2x figures. Excellent plus in good blue and yellow window box. Sold for £160, Vectis, August.

Corgi Toys No 510 Citroën DS Conversion "Tour De France" Team Managers Car, red, yellow interior, grey base with Whizzwheels, grey plastic aerial with "Paramount" to sides. Near mint in good plus blue and yellow window box with "Whizzwheels" flash. Sold for £130, Vectis, August.

Corgi Toys GS13 "Tour De France" Gift Set, white Renault 16 with black bonnet and roof, red interior, cast hubs, black "Paramount" decal, with cameraman and camera, plus cyclist. Excellent, inner polystyrene and display card are excellent in good to good plus blue and yellow window box with pictorial header. Sold for £170, Vectis, August.

Corgi Toys No 479 Commer Van "Samuelson Film Service Limited", two-tone white, blue, cast hubs, with cameraman and camera, black suitcase. Excellent plus, inner carded tray with collectors club folded leaflet is near mint, outer blue and yellow window box is good with pictorial header. Sold for £130, Vectis, August.

Corgi Toys No 1105 Bedford TK Carrimore Car Transporter, red cab, lemon interior, silver trim, spun hubs, with blue and pale green trailer, silver platform, spun hubs. Good plus to excellent in fair to good blue and yellow lift off lid box with inner packing piece, with correct instruction/collectors club folded leaflet, plus excellent "Mr Retailer" card. Sold for £90, Vectis, August.

Corgi Rockets D917 Alfa Romeo P35 Pininfarina, metallic purple, white including spoiler, with key. Near mint on good blister card. Sold for £50, Vectis, August.

Corgi Rockets D903 Mercedes 280SL, metallic blue, off-white interior, with key. Mint on excellent blister card. Sold for £90, Vectis, August.

Corgi Rockets D901 Aston Martin DB6, gold body, green tinted windows, with key. Near mint on good plus blister card. Sold for £50, Vectis, August.

Dinky Toys No 212 Ford Cortina Rally Car, off-white, black bonnet, red interior, chrome spun hubs, roof light, racing number 8. Excellent plus in excellent yellow and red carded box. Sold for £80, Vectis, August.

Dinky Toys No 205 Lotus Cortina Rally Car "Rallye Monte Carlo", white body, red bonnet, boot and stripes, pale blue interior, racing number 7, 2 white plastic aerials, cast spun hubs. Excellent in excellent plus carded picture box. Sold for £110, Vectis, August.

Dinky Toys No 189 Triumph Herald Saloon, two-tone white, light blue, silver trim, chrome spun hubs with black treaded tyres. Excellent plus in good plus plain yellow and red carded box with dark blue colour spot. Sold for £100, Vectis, August.

Corgi Rockets "The Saint's" Volvo P1800, white body, blue interior and bonnet label, with key. Near mint on excellent blister card. Sold for £60, Vectis, August.

Corgi Toys No 311 3-Litre Ford Capri, pink with red spot hubs. Near mint in near mint box. Sold for £100, Lacy Scott & Knight, August.

Corgi Toys No 313 Ford Cortina, bronze, complete with Graham Hill figure. Near mint in a mint original window style box, with Corgi club leaflet. Sold for £120, Lacy Scott & Knight, August.

Corgi Toys No 281 Rover 2000TC, purple with Whizzwheels. Mint in near mint to mint box, with Corgi Club leaflet. Sold for £160, Lacy Scott & Knight, August.

Corgi Toys No 260 Renault 16, metallic red complete with the original clear plastic strips to prop bonnet and boot open for display purposes. Mint in near mint to mint box. Sold for £70, Lacy Scott & Knight, August.

Corgi Toys Whizzwheels No 681 Stunt Motorbike, with Batman sticker still on rider. Mint in near mint to mint box. Sold for £110, Lacy Scott & Knight, August.

Corgi Toys No 471 Smiths Karrier Mobile Canteen, blue body and spun hubs. Near mint to mint in near mint to mint box. Sold for £210, Lacy Scott & Knight, August.

Corgi Toys No 452 Commer 5 Ton Dropside Lorry, red cab and cream bed. Near mint to mint in near mint to mint box, with Corgi paper slip. Sold for £320, Lacy Scott & Knight, August.

Corgi Toys No 428 Smiths ice cream van "Mister Softtee", cream and blue body with spun hubs. Near mint to mint in near mint box, with Corgi paper slip. Sold for £240, Lacy Scott & Knight, August.

Dinky Toys No 35B Trade box of 6 Midget Racers, all finished in silver and red, with tan driver. Very good in very good original buff coloured and labelled trade box, with original dividers. Sold for £200, Lacy Scott & Knight, August.

Dinky Toys No 230 Talbot Lago racing car, blue with racing No 4 and white driver, with grey tyres and yellow plastic hubs. Near mint to mint in near mint box. Sold for £400, Lacy Scott & Knight, August.

Corgi Aviation Archive AA32601 1/72 scale Avro Lancaster, R5868/'PO-S 467 Squadron markings with accessories. Mint condition in excellent inner polystyrene tray within a good lift off lid box. Sold for £55, British Toy Auctions, September.

Corgi Aviation Archive AA34801 1/72 scale Vickers Wellington MK.IA, No 9 Sqn RAF Honnington December 1939 with accessories and wheels. Mint condition in very good lift off lid box. Sold for £40, British Toy Auctions, September.

Corgi Aviation Archive 1/72 scale AA32602 'Battle of Britain Memorial Flight Set', Avro Lancaster EE176 'Mickey the Moocher', Spitfire Mk.IIa P7350 and Hawker Hurricane LF363. Near mint in excellent polystyrene inner box and good outer lift off lid box. Sold for £60, British Toy Auctions, September.

Corgi Aviation Archive 1/144 scale AA37002 Vickers VC-10, G-ARVM, British Airways, London Heathrow Airport 1977. Mint in excellent lift off lid box with excellent outer sleeve. Sold for £40, British Toy Auctions, September.

Dinky Toys No 981 Horse Box 'British Railways Express Horse Box Hire Service', maroon body, silver trim, with three plastic unassociated horses. Fair plus to good overall condition in poor to fair blue and white striped lift off lid box. Sold for £25, British Toy Auctions, September.

Dinky Toys No 439 Ford D800 tipper truck and snow plough, metallic blue cab, with opening doors, and light blue tipper body and metal wheels. Very good in good box. Sold for £28, British Toy Auctions, September.

Autoart No 87183 1/18 scale Steve McQueen Racing Porsche 917K Le Mans, in Gulf livery. Mint in good box. Sold for £130, British Toy Auctions, September.

Gilbow No 991031/24 scale Daimler London DMS Bus, London Transport Catford Garage Routes 108B,124, 124A and 185, with 'Pearl Assurance' advertising, rotating blinds, opening engine cover and Emergency Exit. Mint in polystyrene inner tray with corner protectors and original ribbons, in good box. Sold for £240, British Toy Auctions, September.

Corgi Toys No 441 Volkswagen Toblerone Van, light blue. Good to very good in good box. Sold for £60, Excalibur Auctions, September.

Corgi Toys No 356 VW Military Personnel Carrier, drab olive green. Very good in good to very good box. Sold for £90, Excalibur Auctions, September.

Corgi Toys No 354 Commer Military Ambulance, drab olive green. Very good in good to very good box. Sold for £75, Excalibur Auctions, September.

Corgi Toys No 359 Commer Army Field Kitchen, drab olive green. Very good in good to very good box. Sold for £100, Excalibur Auctions, September.

Corgi Toys No 317 Monte-Carlo 1964 Mini-Cooper S, red, numbered 37. Good to very good in good box. Sold for £95, Excalibur Auctions, September.

Dinky Toys No 134 Triumph Vitesse, blue with red interior. Very good in good box. Sold for £48, Excalibur Auctions, September.

Corgi Toys No 246 Chrysler Imperial, red with pale blue interior, with passengers and golf trolley. Very good in good to very good box. Sold for £55, Excalibur Auctions, September.

Corgi Toys No 231 Triumph Herald Coupe, gold/white. Fair to good in good box. Sold for £42, Excalibur Auctions, September.

Corgi Major Toys No 1126 Ecurie Ecosse Racing Car Transporter, metallic dark blue. Good to very good in good box with internal packing pieces. Sold for £110, Excalibur Auctions, September.

Corgi Toys No 341 Mini Marcos GT850, maroon. Very good in good box. Sold for £38, Excalibur Auctions, September.

Corgi Toys No 327 MGB GT, dark red. Very good in good to very good box. Sold for £50, Excalibur Auctions, September.

Corgi Toys No 221 Chevrolet New York TAXI Cab, deep yellow with red interior, TAXI sign to roof, aerial to rear wing, smooth spun wheels with black tyres. Mint in near mint box. Sold for £130, Wallis & Wallis, September.

Corgi Toys No 218 Aston Martin DB4, yellow with red interior, closed bonnet vent, detailed cast wheels with black tyres. Mint in excellent box. Sold for £100, Wallis & Wallis, September.

Corgi Major Toys No 1101 Carrimore Car Transporter, Big Bedford ('S' Type) tractor unit in mid blue with deep yellow transporter and silver tracks, "Corgi Car Transporter" in deep blue to sides, with Corgi logo to drop down ramp. Good to very good in very good box. Sold for £110, Wallis & Wallis, September.

Corgi Toys No 453 Commer 'Wall's' Refrigerator Van, lighter blue cab and chassis, cream rear body with "Wall's Ice Cream More Than Just A Treat - a food" decals to sides, with smooth spun wheels and black tyres. Very good in very good box. Sold for £170, Wallis & Wallis, September.

French Dinky Toys No 22A Maserati Sport 2000, gloss deep red, ridged plated wheels with black rubber tyres, complete with driver. Mint in excellent box. Sold for £55, Wallis & Wallis, September.

French Dinky Toys No 24H Mercedes-Benz 190SL, off-white with black roof, plated ridged wheels with black rubber tyres. Very good in very good box. Sold for £40, Wallis & Wallis, September.

French Dinky Toys No 25CG Citroën Camionnette 1200 Kg, in C.H.Gervais cream livery, with black tyres and ridged cream wheels. Very good in very good box. Sold for £95, Wallis & Wallis, September.

French Dinky Toys No 25C Camionnette Citroën 1200Kg, in turquoise CIBIE livery with bright yellow dished wheels and black tyres. Very good in very good box. Sold for £100, Wallis & Wallis, September.

Dinky Toys No 25s 6-Wheeled Wagon, reddish brown with grey tin tilt, with holes in seat, complete with driver, smooth wheels with thicker axles and original white rubber tyres. Good. Sold for £40, Wallis & Wallis, September.

Dinky Toys No 22f Army Tank, grey lead body, 'Dinky Toys' cast in, with black rubber tracks. Very good. Sold for £260, Wallis & Wallis, September.

Dinky Toys No 431 Guy Warrior, light brown with dark green rear body, with mid green wheels and black treaded tyres. Boxed, some wear/surface marking. Vehicle very good to mint, very minor chip. Sold for £320, Wallis & Wallis, September.

Dinky Toys No 256 Humber Hawk Police Car, black with cream interior, sign to roof, aerial to drivers side front wing, 'PC 49' number plates, dished spun wheels with black treaded tyres. Mint in near mint box. Sold for £110, Wallis & Wallis, September.

Dinky Austin A40 van in Omnisport livery, One of a very limited number produced by Alan Morris using a genuine Dinky casting, with the correct decals and finished in the correct shade of light blue, colour matched from the original. Mint in reproduction fictional box. Sold for £75, Wallis & Wallis, September.

Dinky Pre-war Set No 42, containing "Police" Telephone Box, Motorcycle Patrol, 2x figures. Good Plus in good plus blue lift off lid box, inner pictorial stand is excellent. Sold for £400, Vectis, September.

Dinky Pre-war 156 "Mechanised Army" Set, contains 151a Medium Tank, 151 Transport Wagon, 151c Cooker Trailer, 151d Water Tank Trailer, 152a Light Tank, 152b Reconnaissance Car, 152c Austin Seven Car, 161a Searchlight Lorry, 161b Anti-Aircraft Gun, 162a Light Dragon and 162c Quick Firing Field Gun - all finished in green with smooth hubs, black wheels and metal tracks. Good to good plus on good carded base in good box with fair lift-off lid. Sold for £2200, Vectis, September.

Dinky Toys No 908 Mighty Antar with Transformer, yellow unit with windows, red Supertoy hubs, light grey trailer with red ramps and Supertoy hubs, with dark grey transformer plastic load with electrodes. Excellent plus with some inner packing pieces in good plus to excellent yellow and red lift-off-lid box. Sold for £520, Vectis, September.

Dinky Toys No 514 Guy (1st Type) "Weetabix" Van, yellow including Supertoy hubs with smooth tyres, silver trim. Good plus to excellent in fair to good blue lift-off-lid box with paper label. Sold for £800, Vectis, September.

Dinky Toys No 920 Guy (Type 3) "Heinz 57 Varieties", red cab and chassis, yellow back and Supertoy hubs with black treaded tyres, silver trim. Excellent in fair to good correct plain blue and white striped box. Sold for £520, Vectis, September.

Dinky Toys No 923 Big Bedford "Heinz 57 Varieties", sauce bottle issue red cab and chassis, yellow back and Supertoy hubs with grey treaded tyres, silver trim. Good plus in good plus blue and white striped lift-off-lid box. Sold for £520, Vectis, September.

Dinky Toys No 935 Leyland Octopus Flat Truck with chains, green cab and chassis, light grey back and cab flashes, red plastic hubs with black treaded tyres, metal tow hook. Good plus to excellent in good box. Sold for £640, Vectis, September.

Matchbox Lesney large scale Massey Harris Tractor, red, cream including hubs, gold trim. Excellent in good carded picture box. Sold for £520, Vectis, September.

Hot Wheels "Rrrumblers" Gift Set, comprises Centurion, Rip Code, Bone Shaker, Preying Menace and Talor. Near mint to mint in near mint plastic tray and excellent plus outer window box, with outer transit brown plain sleeve. Sold for £1300, Vectis, September.

Dinky Toys No 38e Armstrong Siddeley Coupe trade pack, containing 6 examples - 3x green, grey interior and tonneau, mid-green ridged hubs with black smooth tyres and 3x grey including ridged hubs, blue interior and tonneau. Good plus to excellent plus in fair trade box with original dividers. Sold for £420, Vectis, September.

Matchbox Models of Yesteryear Y7 1918 4 Ton Leyland Van "W & R Jacob & Co Ltd", dark brown body and chassis, cream roof, silver radiator shell, grenadised solid wheels, crimped axles, bare metal underside of roof, with rare 2-line decal to near-side of van, Excellent in good type A box. Sold for £380, Vectis, September.

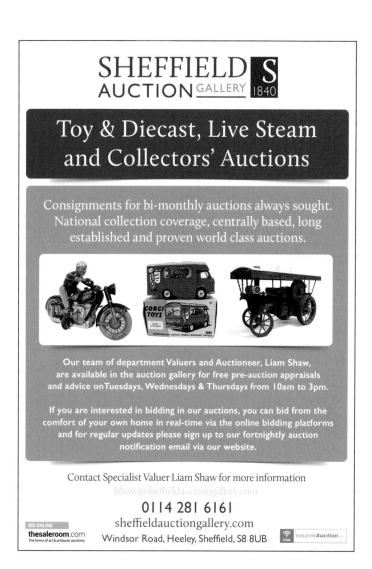
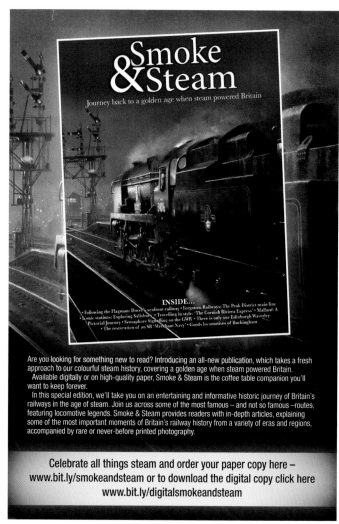

Introduction to Model Railways

Dating back to the middle of the 19th century, model railways have been delighting children and adults for decades. The opportunity to create a working miniature railway in your bedroom, loft or shed (for those collectors forced outside the comforts of the house) is an evocative one. As a result, model railways continue to capture the attention of collectors and prices keep on soaring!

With model railways dating back so long, one of the easiest ways to tell the age of your example, is its method of locomotion. The first model railways were made in brass and fuelled by methylated spirit, or were simple push-along examples. As technology advanced, so too did model railways and from the late 19th century to the 1940s manufacturers switched to clockwork, with the likes of

Bassett-Lowke and Marklin making a name for themself. After the '40s companies began experimenting with electric power and this quickly became the design of choice.

Interestingly, despite the fact that modern model railways have all-manner of fancy technology (such as sound effects and lighting) the locos of yesteryear often fetch a higher price than their modern equivalents!

If you're just starting out in the world of model railways, you might be confused by phrases such as 'N-scale' or 'HO gauge'. Put simply, this refers to the size of the model and how big it is compared to the real thing. Across the globe, descriptions of scale differ slightly but in the UK the main scales are N-scale, HO, OO or O, with N being the smallest. You may also find reference to Z-scale, which is even smaller than N scale, and TT scale, which was introduced

by manufacturer Tri-ang in 1957 but dropped in favour of N scale. Britain is fairly unique in world of model railway collecting because the loading gauge is narrower and lower than in the rest of Europe, meaning that manufacturers used their own distinctive railway scales - something to bear in mind when you're buying European or American locomotives.

Something else to note are the strings of seemingly random numbers in descriptions, such as '4-6-2', '4-6-0' or '2-6-4'. Instead of relating to the scale, this is simply a description of the way the wheels are positioned, with the numbers representing front-middle-rear positions.

But it's not just the gloriously detailed locos that cause a stir at auctions and collectors are also

keen to pick up the numerous coaches and wagons produced by the likes of Hornby, Trix, Marklin and Graham Farish, among others. In fact, some of the particularly rare examples can make just as much as the locomotives that tow them - as you'll see in the pages ahead. What's more, there's also a huge market for the numerous trackside accessories produced, with Marklin stations in particular commanding some very impressive prices at auction throughout the year.

What's more there's also a huge community of collectors that display their vintage railway layouts at events across the country, so keep checking the *Collectors Gazette* to find a club in your area and meet like-minded enthusiasts. ■

A Wrenn WF200 BR Freight train set. Good to very good in a good box. Sold for £220, Excalibur Auctions, November.

A Wrenn WPG300 mixed passenger and goods train set. Good to very good in a good box. Sold for £200, Excalibur Auctions, November.

A Wrenn W2219 Class 4MT 2-6-4 standard tank in LMS maroon numbered 2679. Good to very good in good to very good box. Sold for £75, Excalibur Auctions, November.

A Wrenn W2218 Class 4MT 2-6-4 standard tank in BR black numbered 80033. Good to very good in good to very good box. Sold for £60, Excalibur Auctions, November.

A Wrenn W2229 Duchess class steam locomotive in BR blue "City of Glasgow". Very good in a good to very good box. Sold for £70, Excalibur Auctions, November.

A Wrenn W2219 Class 4MT 2-6-4 standard tank in LMS maroon numbered 2679. Good to very good in good to very good box. Sold for £65, Excalibur Auctions, November.

A Wrenn W4652P Auto Distributors Low Mac wagon with car and caravan. Very good in a good box. Sold for £95, Excalibur Auctions, November.

A Wrenn W2201 Class R1 steam tank locomotive in 'ESSO' blue livery - numbered 38. Very good in a good to very good box. Sold for £100, Excalibur Auctions, November.

A Wrenn W2214 0-6-2 tank locomotive in LMS maroon numbered 2274. Very good in a good to very good box. Sold for £65, Excalibur Auctions, November.

A Wrenn W2237 re-built Bulleid Pacific steam locomotive in Southern Railways Malachite Green 'Lyme Regis'. Very good in a good to very good box. Sold for £130, Excalibur Auctions, November.

A Wrenn W6012A 1st Class Pullman Car - with Golden Arrow logos 'Cecelia' with white tables. Very good in a good to very good box. Sold for £60, Excalibur Auctions, November.

A Wrenn W6012A 1st Class Pullman Car - with Golden Arrow logos 'Cecelia' with white tables. Very good in a good to very good box. Sold for £65, Excalibur Auctions, November.

A Wrenn W6002/H 1st Class Pullman Car 'Hazel' with white tables. Very good in a good to very good box. Sold for £70, Excalibur Auctions, November.

A Wrenn W2230 Bo-Bo Diesel locomotive in BR green livery D8017. Good in a good to very good box. Sold for £45, Excalibur Auctions, November.

A Wrenn W2204 0-6-0 tank locomotive in LMS red numbered 7420. Good to very good in good to very good box. Sold for £48, Excalibur Auctions, November.

Boxed Hornby OO gauge R665 Eurostar Train Pack, complete with Class 373 Powered Locomotive, Class 373 Unpowered Locomotive and 2 x Passenger Saloons. Sold for £75, Wessex Auction Rooms, December.

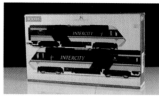

Boxed Hornby OO gauge R2702 DCC Ready BR Intercity Executive Class 43 HST complete with all parts. Sold for £150, Wessex Auction Rooms, December.

Boxed Hornby OO gauge R332 High Speed Train Pack, complete with all parts. Sold for £42, Wessex Auction Rooms, December.

Boxed Hornby OO gauge R3229 DCC Ready BR 4-6-0 Star Class British Monarchy locomotive. Sold for £55, Wessex Auction Rooms, December.

Boxed Hornby OO gauge R2339 LNER 4-6-2 Class A4 Mallard locomotive, tatty outer box. Sold for £55, Wessex Auction Rooms, December.

Boxed ltd edn Hornby OO gauge DCC Ready Super Detail GWR Dean Single 4-2-2 Duke of Edinburgh 3064 locomotive. Sold for £55, Wessex Auction Rooms, December.

Boxed Hornby OO gauge R174 Rural Rambler Set, complete with 1977 catalogue. Sold for £28, Wessex Auction Rooms, December.

Boxed Hornby OO gauge R1048 Western Pullman, electric train set, complete. Sold for £70, Wessex Auction Rooms, December.

Boxed Hornby OO gauge Live Steam Silver Link LNER 4-6-2 Class A4 steam powered locomotive, complete and excellent, with OO Live Steam DVD. Sold for £320, Wessex Auction Rooms, December.

Boxed Tri-ang OO gauge RS37 train set with Davy Crockett Locomotive and tender, two coaches and track plus a boxed Hornby R089 Signal Extension Set and boxed Hornby R087 Junction Signals Set. Sold for £80, Wessex Auction Rooms, December.

Boxed Hornby OO gauge R1085 Local Freight electric train set, complete and very good. Sold for £36, Wessex Auction Rooms, December.

Boxed Hornby Dublo EDLT20 Bristol Castle Locomotive & Tender good, some age wear. Sold for £75, Wessex Auction Rooms, December.

A modified Bassett-Lowke 0 Gauge 2-rail electric 'Standard' 0-6-0 Tank Locomotive, in red-lined black livery with large numbers 5374 to side tanks, outside cylinders with outside Walschaerts valve gear, the mechanism with additional reduction gear for slow running and converted to 2-rail, good, 3-link couplers fitted, rear B-L transfer painted out, a few small chips to paintwork. Sold for £340, Special Auction Services, December.

A Bing for Bassett-Lowke 0 Gauge clockwork LNWR 4-4-0 Tank Locomotive, in red and white-lined LNWR black as no 3611, with original Bing mechanism and bogie, good, mech tested okay, slight crazing to varnish, moderate wear. Sold for £150, Special Auction Services, December.

A Bing for Bassett-Lowke 0 Gauge clockwork LMS 4-4-0 Tank Locomotive, in lined LMS crimson as no 4201, with original Bing mechanism and bogie, good, mech tested okay, slight crazing to varnish, some flaking/chipping of paintwork. Sold for £100, Special Auction Services, December.

A Bing for Bassett-Lowke 0 Gauge clockwork 'George the Fifth' 4-4-0 Locomotive and Tender, in lined LMS crimson as no 5320, with original Bing mechanism and wheels, B-L trademarks to underside of loco body and rear of tender, very good, mech tested okay, some very minor chipping of paintwork around cab roof, together with a suitable key. Sold for £150, Special Auction Services, December.

A Bing for Bassett-Lowke 0 Gauge clockwork 'Compound' 4-4-0 Locomotive and Tender, in lithographed lined LMS crimson as no 1190, with original Bing mechanism and wheels, B-L trademark to rear of tender, good, mech tested okay, several small areas of chipping especially to dome, one or two small retouches and very slight fading to boiler. Sold for £150, December, Special Auction Services.

A Bassett-Lowke 0 Gauge 3-rail electric 'Compound' 4-4-0 Locomotive and Tender, in lithographed lined LMS crimson as no 1108, with original DC electric mechanism, B-L trademark to rear of tender, good, moderate playwear, paint loss from dome and upper cab sides, some crazing to varnish. Sold for £110, December, Special Auction Services.

A Bassett-Lowke 0 Gauge 3-rail electric 'Compound' 4-4-0 Locomotive and Tender, in lithographed lined BR black as no 41109, post-war version with small keyhole to body, appears to be original DC electric mechanism, printed grey B-L trademark to rear of tender, very good, 3 small scratches to top of boiler/firebox. Sold for £160, December, Special Auction Services.

A Bassett-Lowke 0 Gauge 3-rail electric LMS 4-4-2 Tank Locomotive, the LNWR-style locomotive in enamelled lined LMS crimson as no 6810, with original worm-drive mechanism and bogies, good to very good, body possibly over-varnished, some chipping of paintwork to dome, very slight depression to cab roof, bright metal parts grubby. Sold for £290, December, Special Auction Services.

A Bassett-Lowke 0 Gauge 3-rail electric 'Princess Elizabeth' 4-4-0 Locomotive and Tender, an uncommon original electric version in lithographed LMS crimson as no 2265, body without keyhole, good to very good, lithography generally good with bright gold lettering, moderate chipping/scratches to footplate edges and some other areas. Sold for £130, December, Special Auction Services.

A Leeds for Bassett-Lowke 0 Gauge clockwork Caledonian Railway 'Pickersgill Class 72' 4-4-0 Locomotive and Tender, in lined Caledonian blue as no 77, with original mechanism and wheels, fair to good, mech tested okay, fall plate detached from mountings, brake control knob missing, slight damage to front end footplate/frame (left side), paintwork and transfers mostly intact but general deterioration of varnish coat throughout (3 inc loose fall-plate). Sold for £1850, December, Special Auction Services.

A Bing for Bassett-Lowke 0 Gauge clockwork 'Prince of Wales' 4-6-0 Locomotive and Tender, in enamelled lined LMS crimson as no 5600, with original Bing direct-wind 6-coupled mechanism, good to very good, mech tested okay, some damage to left side cab steps area, a few small chips elsewhere, the whole body and tender appear quite thickly gloss varnished which may or may not be original. Sold for £850, December, Special Auction Services.

A Bing for Bassett-Lowke 0 Gauge clockwork 'Ivatt Atlantic' 4-4-2 Locomotive and Tender, in enamelled lined GNR green with brown frames as no 1442, with original Bing mechanism, very good, mech tested okay, slight damage to tender coal rails, complete with key (3 inc key). Sold for £850, December, Special Auction Services.

Bassett-Lowke O Gauge 4-6-2 Loco and Tender LMS maroon Duchess Class "Duchess of Montrose" No.6232, 3-rail electric. Loco appears to have had little running, additional weights professionally added to the front bogie and rear pony units, line of black overpainting to the underside of the rear of the cab roof. Tender couplings refixed and additional weight added to the tender. Overall paint work is excellent to excellent plus all contained in a good plus box with instructions. Sold for £700, Vectis, January.

Bassett-Lowke O Gauge 4-6-0 Loco and Tender LMS black "Royal Scot" No.6100 3-rail electric. Locomotive front and tender rear couplings refixed. Loco appears little used near mint in excellent box with instructions. Sold for £950, Vectis, January.

Bassett-Lowke O Gauge 2-6-4 LMS Stanier Tank lined black No.2603 3-rail electric. Some light wear to some edges, coal added to bunker back otherwise excellent to excellent plus, tear to box lid corner otherwise excellent and includes instructions. Sold for £500, Vectis, January.

Bassett-Lowke O Gauge 2-6-0 Loco and Tender LMS lined black No.2945 3-rail electric. Possibly from a steam body this loco and tender have been repainted, lined and transferred with running number 2945 to cab side and LMS lettering to tender sides. Coal has been added to the tender contained in a excellent Bassett-Lowke "Mogul" box. Sold for £340, Vectis, January.

Bassett-Lowke or similar O Gauge 4-6-0 Loco and Tender Great Western lined green Castle Class "Dunster Castle" No.4093. 6-coupled Bassett-Lowke mechanism and finished in lined GWR green with Dunster Castle, running number 4093 to cab side and Great Crest Western to tender sides. In a Bassett-Lowke LMS Duchess box. Excellent. Sold for £750, Vectis, January.

Bachmann OO Gauge 32-850Z (Limited Edition) 2-10-0 BR black 9F Class Loco No.92240 complete with certificate No.157 of 504 produced for Modelzone, this is a factory weathered edition, condition excellent in generally good to good plus box. Sold for £120, Vectis, January.

Bachmann OO Gauge 31-921 4-4-2 BR lined black (ex LBSCR) H2 Atlantic Class No.32424 "Beachy Head" complete with a pack of etched nameplates for optional fitment, condition excellent plus to near mint in excellent plus to near mint box. Sold for £130, Vectis, January.

Bachmann OO Gauge 31-460 0-6-0 South East & Chatham Railway lined green livery C Class No.952 front coupling not fitted but is in box with other detailing items, condition near mint to mint in excellent plus to near mint box. Sold for £160, Vectis, January.

OO Gauge Kitbuilt DJH K41 4-6-2 BR green Britannia Class No.70033 "Charles Dickens", small paint chip to left side smoke deflector and centre sand box on left side running plate, professionally built and painted, condition excellent. Sold for £130, Vectis, January.

OO Gauge Kitbuilt 4-6-2 LNER black A7 Class Tank Loco No.1170 fitted with portescap type motor, nicely built and painted, condition good plus Sold for £130, Vectis, January.

OO Gauge Kitbuilt 4-4-2 GWR green De Glehn Compound Loco No.103 "President", superbly built and painted with excellent detail, condition excellent. Sold for £180, Vectis, January.

OO Gauge Kitbuilt 0-4-2 LNWR plain black Box Tank No.3473 fitted with portescap type motor, right side cab footstep detached but is in box, nicely built and painted, condition excellent. Sold for £130, Vectis, January.

OO Gauge Kitbuilt DJH 2-8-0 BR black WD Austerity Class No.90074, professionally built and painted, condition excellent. Sold for £140, Vectis, January.

OO Gauge Kitbuilt DJH K85 4-6-2 BR green rebuilt Battle of Britain Class Loco No.34085 "501 Squadron", fitted with portescap type motor, superbly built and painted, condition excellent. Sold for £140, Vectis, January.

Bassett-Lowke O gauge electric BR green 62453 Prince Charles locomotive No. 4311/0. Good condition but without a box. Sold for £80, Warwick and Warwick, January.

Hornby O gauge clockwork (without key) LNER green 234 Yorkshire 4-4-0 locomotive No. 2 Special generally excellent in excellent reproduction box. Sold for £180, Warwick and Warwick, January.

Hornby O gauge clockwork (without key) LMS maroon 6100 Royal Scot locomotive No. 3C generally excellent in excellent reproduction box. Sold for £90, Warwick and Warwick, January.

Hornby Dublo OO gauge Metro-Vic (Class 28) Diesel Co-Bo 2-rail BR D5702 green locomotive No. 2233 about mint in good plus box with instructions. Sold for £100, Warwick and Warwick, January.

Hornby Dublo OO gauge Class AL1 (Class 81) AC Electric Bo-Bo BR E3002 blue locomotive No. 2245 about mint in excellent box with packing piece. Sold for £360, Warwick and Warwick, January.

Ace Trains O Gauge BRb green 70000 Britannia 4-6-2 locomotive and tender No E27A mint in excellent box. Sold for £650, Warwick and Warwick, January.

F.M. Models (Korea) O Gauge BR green 92220 Evening Star 9f Class 2-10-0 locomotive and tender, additionally fitted with Loksound V4.0 Decoder and smoke unit, mint in about mint box, with copy of original 2016 receipt. Sold for £1300, Warwick and Warwick, January.

A Wrenn W2207 R1 class steam tank locomotive in SR Green, numbered 1127, very good in a good to very good box. Sold for £50, Excalibur Auctions, January.

A Wrenn 2218 2-6-4 steam tank locomotive, in BR black, numbered 80033, good in a good box. Sold for £50, Excalibur Auctions, January.

A Wrenn 2221 Castle Class steam locomotive 'Cardiff Castle', in BR green, good to very good in a fair to good period 1 box. Sold for £60, Excalibur Auctions, January.

A Wrenn 2224 Class 8F steam locomotive, in BR black, numbered 48073, good in fair to good box. Sold for £55, Excalibur Auctions, January.

A Wrenn 2235 West Country Class steam locomotive, in BR green livery 'Barnstaple', good to very good in good period 1 box. Sold for £85, Excalibur Auctions, January.

A Wrenn W2205 Class R1 steam tank locomotive, in BR black livery, good to very good in good box. Sold for £38, Excalibur Auctions, January.

Hornby R3461 DCC Digital (Tested OK) #07 LNER Thompson L1, boxed with instructions and detail pack. Sold for £65, Warrington & Northwich Auction, February.

Hornby R3663TTS DCC Digital (Tested OK) #09 Tornado, with sound, boxed with instructions and detail pack. Sold for £80, Warrington & Northwich Auction, February.

Hornby R3603TTS DCC Digital (Tested OK) #05 BR Lord Nelson, with sound, boxed with instructions and detail pack. Sold for £120, Warrington & Northwich Auction, February.

Hornby R3385TTS DCC Digital (Tested OK) #06 BR Class 5 45116, with sound, boxed with instructions and detail pack. Sold for £110, Warrington & Northwich Auction, February.

Hornby 'Flying Scotsman' Train Set 'Locomotive, boxed. Sold for £55, Warrington & Northwich Auction, February.

Hornby R2108 Class 155 BR Sprinter, boxed. Sold for £50, Warrington & Northwich Auction, February.

Hornby R1183 'Master of the Glens' Train Set, boxed with instructions, and an upgraded black/red controller. Sold for £85, Warrington & Northwich Auction, February.

Hornby R1169 'Tornado Pullman Express' Train Set, boxed with instructions. Sold for £85, Warrington & Northwich Auction, February.

Hornby R3285TTS Gadwell, boxed with instructions and detail pack. Sold for £90, Warrington & Northwich Auction, February.

Hornby R2141 'Isambard Kingdom Brunei' BR, boxed, detailpack already fitted. Sold for £60, Warrington & Northwich Auction, February.

Bachmann 31-475 G2A BR Early NRM Issue, boxed with instructions, but lacking detail pack. Sold for £55, Warrington & Northwich Auction, February.

Bachmann DCC Digital (Tested Set to #03) #32-000DC 'Guild Hall', boxed with instructions and detail pack. Sold for £60, Warrington & Northwich Auction, February.

Hornby R2204 Merchant Navy, boxed (but box torn) with instructions, but lacking detail pack. Sold for £70, Warrington & Northwich Auction, February.

Hornby R2280 'Blenheim Castle', boxed with instructions, but lacking detail pack. Sold for £50, Warrington & Northwich Auction, February.

Bachmann 32-479 Class 40 169, Centre Head Code (w/o tanks), boxed with instructions and detail pack. Sold for £60, Warrington & Northwich Auction, February.

Bachmann 32-426 Class 24, plain BR green loco with detail pack, instructions and box. Sold for £65, Warrington & Northwich Auction, February.

Bachmann 31-554 V2 Doube Chimney Loco, boxed, no detail pack or instructions. Sold for £50, Warrington & Northwich Auction, February.

Hornby R2201 'Robert the Devil' Loco, with detail pack, no instructions and boxed. Sold for £60, Warrington & Northwich Auction, February.

Hornby R2015 'City of Hereford' Loco, with detail pack, instructions and boxed. Lacking a handrail on boiler. Sold for £45, Warrington & Northwich Auction, February.

Hornby R2170 'Holland - Afrika Line' Merchant Navy Loco, boxed, no detail pack or Instructions. Side step missing. Sold for £70, Warrington & Northwich Auction, February.

Bachmann 31-854 J39, BR Black E/Emblem weathered anddetailed loco, with instructions and box. Sold for £40, Warrington & Northwich Auction, February.

Hornby R2152 '60085 MANNA' Loco, with detail pack, instructions and box. Sold for £65, Warrington & Northwich Auction, February.

Wrenn N Gauge Micro Model Set 2, a boxed freight set includes electric Bo-Bo E3185 with pantograph, four goods wagons, track and controller, good, box good. Sold for £70, Special Auction Services, February.

Hornby (China) OO Gauge East Coast Express Train Set, a boxed R1021 set appears complete with Britannia Class, John of Gaunt Steam Locomotive and tender, coaches and accessories including track mat, good to excellent, box with outer box good to excellent. Sold for £100, Special Auction Services, February.

Hornby (China) OO Gauge Atlantic Coast Express Train Pack, a limited edition boxed set R2194 factory packaged includes Merchant Navy Class Holland America Line steam locomotive and tender, three Southern coaches and certificate 1887/2000, excellent, box good. Sold for £110, Special Auction Services, February.

Hornby (China) OO Gauge Atlantic Coast Express Train Pack, a limited edition boxed set R2194 factory packaged includes Merchant Navy Class Holland America Line steam locomotive and tender, three Southern coaches and certificate 472 /2000, excellent, box good. Sold for £110, Special Auction Services, February.

Hornby (China) OO Gauge The Pines Express Train Pack, a limited edition boxed set R2436 factory packaged includes West Country Class Coombe Martin steam locomotive and tender, three maroon coaches and certificate 1386/3000, excellent, box good. Sold for £130, Special Auction Services, February.

Hornby (China) OO Gauge Torbay Express Train Pack, a limited edition boxed set R2090 factory packaged includes Castle Class Llanstephan Castle steam locomotive and tender three crimson and cream coaches and certificate 1172/2000, excellent, box good. Sold for £100, Special Auction Services, February.

Hornby (China) OO Gauge Thames-Clyde Express Train Pack, a boxed R2392M matched set factory packaged includes Dornoch Firth steam locomotive and tender and three maroon coaches, excellent, box good. Sold for £100, Special Auction Services, February.

Hornby (China) OO Gauge Devon Belle Train Pack, a boxed limited edition R2568 set factory packaged includes West Country Class Watersmeet steam locomotive and tender, three Pullman coaches and certificate 1072/2000, excellent, box good. Sold for £150, Special Auction Services, February.

Hornby (China) OO Gauge Golden Arrow Train Pack and Coach Pack, a boxed R2369 set factory packaged includes Battle of Britain Class Golden Arrow steam locomotive and tender and three Pullman coaches, together with R4196 Golden Arrow Coaches includes three Pullman coaches, excellent, boxes good. Sold for £200, Special Auction Services, February.

Hornby (China) OO Gauge Bournemouth Belle Train Pack and Coach Pack, a boxed R2300 set factory packaged includes Merchant Navy Class New Zealand Line steam locomotive and tender and three Pullman coaches, together with R4169 Bournemouth Belle Pullman Cars includes three coaches, excellent, boxes excellent. Sold for £210, Special Auction Services, February.

A Boxed Formo (Graham Farish) 00 Gauge 3-rail Goods Set, with 'Q'-type 0-6-0 locomotive, tender, wagons and circle of track, in original box with all dividers and packing pieces, very good, loco appears never run, slight corrosion to tender wheels, box good, a little discolouring to label. Sold for £100, Special Auction Services, February.

A 7mm Scale 'O' Gauge GWR 57XX Class 0-6-0 Pannier Tank Locomotive, by Minerva, weathered, boxed. Sold for £150, Sheffield Auction Gallery, March.

DIECAST | RAILWAYS | TOY FIGURES | TINPLATE | TV & FILM | OTHERS | EBUYS

A Dapol 'O' Gauge 0-6-0 Class 57xx Locomotive, finished in Great Western, boxed. Sold for £120, Sheffield Auction Gallery, March.

An 'HO' Scale Jouef 'Orient Express' comprising 4-6-2 locomotive 231K with tender, four coaches including 'Wagon', boxed. Sold for £50, Sheffield Auction Gallery, March.

An 'O'/7mm Scale Eight Wheel Kit Based LMS Corridor Coach. Good condition, boxed. Sold for £45, Sheffield Auction Gallery, March.

A 'O'/7mm Scale Eight Wheel LMS 'Porthole' Corridor Coach, kit based, requires a repaint. Sold for £40, Sheffield Auction Gallery, March.

An 'HO' Scale 4-6-2 Class 36 Bavarian Locomotive and Tender by Roco, No. 63371, digital/sound, appears little used/untested, boxed. Sold for £95, Sheffield Auction Gallery, March.

A Piko 'HO' Scale 2-10-0 German BR52 Class Locomotive and Tender, boxed. Sold for £45, Sheffield Auction Gallery, March.

A Leopold Halling 'HOe' Gauge Model No 5090 005-9 Railcar, grey and red finish, boxed. Sold for £95, Sheffield Auction Gallery, March.

A 'OO' Scale Tri-ang Hornby No. R861 - 2-10-0 'Evening Star', boxed. Sold for £40, Sheffield Auction Gallery, March.

A Bachmann 'OO' Gauge Model No 32-277 2-6-0 K3 61949 BR Lined Black, DCC ready, boxed, playworn. Sold for £45, Sheffield Auction Gallery, March.

A Bachmann 'OO' Gauge Model No 32-175 2-6-0 Crab 13098 LMS Crimson, boxed. Sold for £40, Sheffield Auction Gallery, March.

An HO gauge Balboa American outline locomotive. A brass model of a Southern Pacific Co-Co diesel locomotive in orange and red lined livery. Boxed, some flaking to the finish on the lid. Locomotive very good to mint. Sold for £130, Wallis & Wallis, April.

A Tenshodo, Japan, HO gauge Japanese National Railways locomotive (No.475). Brass model for 2-rail running of a Bo-Bo diesel locomotive, DD13 62, in grey, red and white livery. Boxed, minor wear. Very good, very minor paint chipping. Sold for £100, Wallis & Wallis, April.

A Tenshodo, Japan, HO gauge Japanese National Railways locomotive (No.450). A well detailed brass model for 2-rail running of a Bo-Bo diesel locomotive, DF50 502, in black livery. Boxed, minor wear. Locomotive very good, minor paint chipping. Sold for £150, Wallis & Wallis, April.

A Tenshodo, Japan, HO gauge Japanese National Railways locomotive. A well detailed brass model for 2-rail running of a Bo-Bo pantograph locomotive, EF3015, in silver livery. Boxed, minor wear. Locomotive very good, possible minor running wear. Sold for £220, Wallis & Wallis, April.

A United Scale Models, Toyko Japan, HO gauge US outline locomotive. A well detailed metal model for 2-rail running of a Great Northern Railway (box reads Duluth, Missabe and Iron Range Railway) 0-10-2 locomotive with bogie tender in dark green, black and red livery, 790. Boxed, minor wear. Locomotive very good, minor running wear and damage to a few detail parts. Sold for £240, Wallis & Wallis, April.

A United Scale Models, by Atlas Industries Japan, HO gauge US outline locomotive for Pacific Fast Mail. A well detailed brass model for 2-rail running of a Union Pacific 2-8-0 locomotive with bogie tender in unpainted brass. Boxed, minor wear. Locomotive very good, possible minor wear only. Sold for £150, Wallis & Wallis, April.

A United Scale Models, by Atlas Industries Japan, HO gauge US outline locomotive for Pacific Fast Mail. A well detailed brass model for 2-rail running of a Southern Pacific 4-6-2 locomotive with bogie tender, 1401, in green livery. Boxed, minor wear. Locomotive very good, possible minor wear only. Sold for £280, Wallis & Wallis, April.

A United Scale Models, by Atlas Industries Japan, HO gauge US outline locomotive. A well detailed brass model for 2-rail running of a Chesapeake & Ohio Mallet Articulated 2-6-6-2 locomotive with bogie tender in unpainted brass. Boxed, some wear. Locomotive very good, minor wear and discolouration to brass only. Sold for £400, Wallis & Wallis, April.

A scarce Trix OO gauge B.R. type 4 Bo-Bo Warship Class 42 diesel hydraulic Locomotive 'Vanguard', D801. An example in B.R. blue livery with yellow end panels and yellow line to sides. A harder to find example. Very good minor wear for age and type. Sold for £50, Wallis & Wallis, April.

A Lehmann LGB (45mm) Swiss Rhätische Bahn 'Crocodile' electric locomotive. A 6-axle, articulated pantograph locomotive, 413, in brown with double pantograph pick-ups (2040). Boxed, some wear/minor damage. Locomotive good to very good, some running wear and possible minor damage, Sold for £240, Wallis & Wallis, April.

Hornby SR T9 Loco with Detail Pack, instructions, boxed. Sold for £55, Warrington & Northwich Auctions, April.

Hornby Southern Suburban Coaches 1938, boxed. Sold for £50, Warrington & Northwich Auctions, April.

Hornby GWR 2-6-2T Prarie Loco, with instructions, boxed. Sold for £30, Warrington & Northwich Auctions, April.

Hornby 'Blackmoor Vale' 21C123 Loco, with detail pack, instructions, boxed. Sold for £60, Warrington & Northwich Auctions, April.

Rivarossi Royal Scot Loco, boxed. Sold for £40, Warrington & Northwich Auctions, April.

Bachmann N Class SR Loco, with detail pack, instructions, boxed. Sold for £35, Warrington & Northwich Auctions, April.

A 'Z' Gauge Marklin Miniclub No. 8856 'Crocodile' Locomotive, motor removed, but present, boxed. Sold for £50, Sheffield Auction Services, April.

An 'N' Gauge BR Class 101, three car DMU by Graham Farish, boxed. Sold for £70, Sheffield Auction Services, April.

An 'HO' Gauge Liliput 2-10-2 Steam Locomotive R/No 77002, motor appears removed, spares/ repair, boxed. Sold for £28, Sheffield Auction Services, April.

An 'N' Gauge BR Class 101, three car DMU by Graham Farish, boxed. Sold for £80, Sheffield Auction Services, April.

An 'HO' Gauge Roco Class BR 1670 continental 'Electric' Locomotive, used, boxed. Sold for £35, Sheffield Auction Services, April.

A 'OO' Scale Class 33 Locomotive, in BR green, R/No D6583 by Heljan, boxed. Sold for £60, Sheffield Auction Services, April.

An 'HO' Scale American Outline Diesel Locomotive GP38-2 Deleware and Hudson', by Proto 2000 Series, boxed. Sold for £28, Sheffield Auction Services, April.

An 'HO' Scale American Outline GP 30 Diesel, 'Nickel Plate Road', by Spectrum, boxed. Sold for £35, Sheffield Auction Services, April.

A 'OO' Scale Class 26 Locomotive in Railfreight Livery by Heljan Product No 26341, boxed. Sold for £35, Sheffield Auction Services, April.

A coarse scale O gauge scratchbuilt model of a BR Class 35 Bo-Bo Warship diesel locomotive, Sultan D7096, in early BR Brunswick Green livery. A cleverly conceived model incorporating parts from a Tri-ang 'Big Train' Hymek together with scratchbuilt elements to create a convincing model with a good level of detail, sprung buffers, etc. It has a centre 'sleigh' pickup for stud third rail running. Good condition, some running wear and issues with finish/detailing which would benefit from improvement. Sold for £40, Wallis and Wallis, May.

A finescale O gauge kitbuilt model of an LNWR 4-4-2T Webb Metropolitan tank locomotive, 3095, in lined black livery. A well detailed brass model with sprung buffers, etc. Very good. Sold for £180, Wallis and Wallis, May.

A finescale O gauge kitbuilt model of a Midland Railway 4-2-2 Johnson tender locomotive, 1863, in lined maroon livery. A well detailed brass model with sprung buffers, etc. Very good. Sold for £240, Wallis and Wallis, May.

A finescale O gauge kitbuilt model of an LSWR Class 700 0-6-0 Drummond tender locomotive, 687, in lined green livery. A well detailed brass model with sprung buffers, etc. Notes on underside of tender suggest it is for either 2-rail running or third rail stud pickup running. Very good. Sold for £240, Wallis and Wallis, May.

A finescale O gauge kitbuilt model of an LSWR Class X2 4-4-0 Adams tender locomotive, 592, in lined green livery. A well detailed brass model with sprung buffers, etc. Possibly 2-rail running or third rail stud pickup running. Very good. Sold for £240, Wallis and Wallis, May.

A finescale O gauge kitbuilt model of an LBSCR 2-2-2 tender locomotive, Jenny Lind 70, in lined green livery. A well detailed brass model with sprung buffers, etc. For 2-rail running. Together with a contemporary 4-wheel compartment coach. Very good. Sold for £220, Wallis and Wallis, May.

A finescale O gauge kitbuilt model of a GWR Class 32xx 4-4-0 tender locomotive, 3204, in lined green livery. A brass model with some detailing. For 2-rail running. Good, minor running wear and would benefit from minor improvements to finish and paintwork. Sold for £170, Wallis and Wallis, May.

A finescale O gauge kitbuilt model of an LBSCR K Class 2-6-0 tender locomotive, 337, in lined brown livery. A well detailed brass model with sprung buffers, etc. Builder's notes on underside of tender suggest it is for either 2-rail running or third rail stud pickup running (however no pick ups fitted). Fair to good, minor running wear and chassis detached from body. Sold for £220, Wallis and Wallis, May.

A finescale O gauge kitbuilt model of a Pullman Class 73 Bo-Bo diesel locomotive, Brighton Evening Argus 73101, in brown and cream Pullman livery as the locomotive for the Brighton Belle train. A well detailed resin etc model with sprung buffers, etc. With both bogies motored for 2-rail running. Good, minor running wear and would benefit from minor improvements to finish and paintwork. Sold for £180, Wallis and Wallis, May.

A finescale O gauge kitbuilt model of a Somerset & Dorset Joint Railway Class 7F 2-8-0 tender locomotive, 89, in lined dark blue livery. A well detailed brass model with sprung buffers, etc. For third rail stud pickup running (sleigh pick up fitted). Very good, minor running wear. Sold for £540, Wallis and Wallis, May.

A finescale O gauge kitbuilt model of an LNER Class P2 2-8-2 Mikado tender locomotive, Earl Marischal 2002, in lined green livery. A well detailed brass model with sprung buffers, etc. Very good, minor running wear. Sold for £440, Wallis and Wallis, May.

A finescale O gauge kitbuilt model of a Southern Railway Class N15 4-6-0 tender locomotive, Sir Bors de Ganis 763, in lined olive green livery with bogie tender. A well detailed brass model with sprung buffers, etc. Builder's notes on underside of tender suggest it is for either 2-rail running or third rail stud pickup running (sleigh pick up fitted and switch in cab). Very good, minor running wear. Sold for £460, Wallis and Wallis, May.

A live steam, spirit fired O gauge model of a Great Central 4-6-0 tender locomotive. A heavily modified and over painted Bassett Lowke 'Enterprise'. Pot boiler with regulator, 2 cylinders and spirit tank under cab (missing spirit tank and burners). Bassett Lowke label to underside of tender. Locomotive fair, for restoration. Sold for £95, Wallis and Wallis, May.

A live steam O gauge Bowman Models locomotive. Spirit fired 2 cylinder tinplate model of an LNER 4-4-0 locomotive, 4472, in unlined green livery. Together with the remains of the wooden box for the locomotive only. Good condition, running wear, some blistering to paintwork and possible restoration required. Sold for £130, Wallis and Wallis, May.

A live steam O gauge Bowman Models locomotive. Spirit fired 2 cylinder tinplate model of an LMS 4-4-0 locomotive, 13000, in lined maroon livery. Together with the remains of the boxes for the locomotive and tender. Good, running wear. Sold for £170, Wallis and Wallis, May.

A live steam O gauge Bowman Models locomotive. Spirit fired 2 cylinder tinplate model of an LNER 0-4-0T locomotive, 300, in lined green livery. Together with some additional parts for another loco, including a 4-4-0 chassis and spirit tank/burners. Fair to good, running wear, blistering/damage to paintwork, restoration required. Sold for £120, Wallis and Wallis, May.

Hornby. Live steam 31/2" gauge Stephenson's Rocket set, good plus in good plus box and good lid, with Rocket 0-2-2 locomotive and tender (has been fired), plastic track, accessories and instructions, plus coach No. G104 and Track No. G102 (2) in good boxes. Contents appear complete but unchecked. Sold for £160, Warwick & Warwick, May.

Mamod. Live Steam collection generally excellent in excellent boxes, with unmade kit (contents appear complete but unchecked) of Gauge 1 or O (changeable) 0-4-0T SLK1 locomotive No. 1402, straight track pack No. TS1, unboxed O gauge green 0-4-0T locomotive good, No.1322, open wagon, chassis and track. Sold for £220, Warwick & Warwick, May.

O Gauge unboxed collection with Bassett-Lowke LMS maroon 1927 Duke of York 4-4-0, Hornby c/w green 5400 0-4-0 with mismatched tender, BR black 82011 0-4-0T, goods wagons, signal etc, in mixed condition. Sold for £160, Warwick & Warwick, May.

Unboxed tank locomotive range with Wrenn SE&CR green 69 Class R1 0-6-0T, Hornby Dublo BR black 69560 N2 Class 0-6-2T (repainted), Hornby LBSC brown 100 Class E2 0-6-0T, Mainline North Eastern green Joem Terrier 0-6-0T etc good to excellent, some re-painted, re-numbered. Sold for £120, Warwick & Warwick, May.

HORNBY (China) 00 gauge R2196M "The Cambrian Coast Express" Train Pack containing: Castle Class 4-6-0 "Nunney Castle" Loco and Tender No. 5029 GWR lined green, plus 3 GWR chocolate and cream Coaches, all with fitted Coach boards (Paddington, Aberystwyth and Pwhelli), with Certificate No 0271 of 1,500 produced, with paperwork. Excellent plus. Sold for £70, UK Toy & Model Auctions, May.

HORNBY (China) 00 gauge R2600M (DCC Ready) "The Cheltenham Flyer" Train Pack containing: Castle Class 4-6-0 "Tregenna Castle" Loco and Tender No. 5006 GWR lined green, plus 3 GWR chocolate and cream Coaches, Limited Edition with Certificate No. 0551 of 1,500 produced, with paperwork. Excellent plus in excellent plus box. Sold for £70, UK Toy & Model Auctions, May.

HORNBY (China) 00 gauge R2077 "The Merchant Venturer" Train Pack containing: 4-6-0 "Earl Cairns" Loco and Tender No. 5053 BR lined green early crest. Please Note: Loco replaces King Class Loco originally supplied with set, plus 3 GWR chocolate and cream Coaches) all with fitted Coach boards (Paddington, Bath and Weston-Super-Mare). Excellent in excellent box. Sold for £70, UK Toy & Model Auctions, May.

HORNBY (China) 00 gauge GWR Train Pack containing: 4-6-0 "County of Somerset" Loco and Tender No. 1004 GWR lined green, plus 3 GWR chocolate and cream coaches, excellent in a good box. Sold for £65, UK Toy & Model Auctions, May.

HORNBY (China) 00 gauge GWR Train Pack containing: 4-6-0 "Windsor Castle" Loco and Tender No. 4082 GWR lined green – "DCC Fitted Sticker" to base of Loco, plus 3 GWR chocolate and cream Coaches. Excellent in a good Great British Train Pack box. Sold for £70, UK Toy & Model Auctions, May.

HORNBY (China) 00 gauge R2544 (DCC Ready) King Class 4-6-0 "King George I" Loco and Tender No. 6006 GWR lined green with accessory pack and paperwork. Excellent plus in excellent plus box. Sold for £55, UK Toy & Model Auctions, May.

HORNBY (China) 00 gauge R2064 Dean Goods 0-6-0 Loco and Tender No. 2468 GWR green with Paperwork. Excellent plus in good plus box. Sold for £40, UK Toy & Model Auctions, May.

HORNBY (China) 00 gauge R2459 (DCC Ready) Castle Class 4-6-0 "Wellington" Loco and Tender No. 5075 GWR lined green with accessory pack and paperwork. Excellent plus in excellent box. Sold for £55, UK Toy & Model Auctions, May.

HORNBY (China) 00 gauge R2153A Class 2800 2-8-0 Loco and Tender GWR green with accessory pack and paperwork. Excellent plus in excellent plus box. Sold for £40, UK Toy & Model Auctions, May.

HORNBY (China) 00 gauge R2391 County Class 4-6-0 "County of Carnarvon" Loco and Tender No. 1010 GWR lined green with accessory pack and paperwork. Excellent plus in excellent box. Sold for £50, UK Toy & Model Auctions, May.

HORNBY (China) 00 gauge R2064B Dean Goods 0-6-0 Loco and Tender No. 2526 GWR lined green. Excellent plus in a good plus Hornby box with hand-written loco information to end flap. Sold for £35, UK Toy & Model Auctions, May.

HORNBY (China) 00 gauge R2498 (DCC Ready) Castle Class 4-6-0 "Taunton Castle" Loco and Tender No. 7036 BR lined green early crest weathered with accessory pack and paperwork. Excellent plus in excellent plus box. Sold for £50, UK Toy & Model Auctions, May.

HORNBY DUBLO 2-Rail 2235 4-6-2 West Country Loco & Tender BR Green No.34005 'Barnstaple' (coal added). Excellent and boxed (ink stained at one end) with instructions. Sold for £60, UK Toy & Model Auctions, May.

HORNBY DUBLO 2-Rail 2224 2-80-8F Loco & Tender, BR Black No.48073 (coal added). Very good, boxed with instructions. Sold for £60, UK Toy & Model Auctions, May.

BACHMANN '00' 31-152 Jubilee Class Loco & Tender No.45568 'Western Australia' BR Black. Excellent, boxed. Sold for £35, UK Toy & Model Auctions, May.

Marklin HO train set ref. 2920, comprising 0-6-0 tank loco with two open end 4-wheel coaches, track and controller, near mint. Sold for £60, Lacy, Scott & Knight, June.

Marklin HO train set ref. 3200, comprising 0-6-0 tank loco, goods van, tipper wagon and 3-plank open with track, contents excellent to near mint. Sold for £45, Lacy, Scott & Knight, June.

Marklin HO train set ref. 3148, comprising 4-6-2 loco and tender No.01097, one bogie side plate missing from tender, otherwise very good. Sold for £80, Lacy, Scott & Knight, June.

Marklin HO 3089 loco and tender 4-6-2, streamlined, red, No.031055, near mint. Sold for £85, Lacy, Scott & Knight, June.

Marklin HO 3080 0-6-0 diesel shunter loco, yellow with black stripe, excellent. Sold for £30, Lacy, Scott & Knight, June.

A 00 gauge superbly executed model in brass of an LMS/BR Jubilee 4-6-0 locomotive and tender believed to have been professionally manufactured in Japan to a very high standard with lots of extra details such as brake hangers, and pipework, chassis has sprung driving wheel axles, housed in a plastic and foam packed box. Sold for £200, Lacy, Scott & Knight, June.

EDL11 Hornby Dublo Siilver King loco and tender, gloss very good. Sold for £40, Lacy, Scott & Knight, June.

EDP12 Hornby Dublo Duchess of Montrose passenger set, loco and tender, 2 D12 maroon and cream coaches, excellent, box base good. Sold for £45, Lacy, Scott & Knight, June.

Hornby R3457 SR 4-4-0 T9 class no.116, DCC ready, mint. Sold for £60, Lacy, Scott & Knight, June.

A Bachman No. 31-475A British Railways late Crest Class G2A engine and tender, with back cab, housed in the original sliding display box. Sold for £35, Lacy, Scott & Knight, June.

A Hornby Railways model No. R682 The Blue Streak gift set comprising of Sir Nigel Gresley locomotive with three LNER teak coaches, supplied with a quantity of track and transformer, contents appear incomplete but the majority are present. Sold for £55, Lacy, Scott & Knight, June.

Dapol 4D-022-008 Class 68 diesel electric loco 68003 Astute DRS Early Service. Excellent but missing some internal fitments. Sold for £75, Lacy, Scott & Knight, June.

Wrenn W2301 LMS streamlined "Coronation" loco and tender, 6221 "Queen Elizabeth", one small chip to base of L/H cabside, otherwise mint. Sold for £320, Lacy, Scott & Knight, June.

A Bachmann 32-603 Class 220 Cross Country four car DMU, housed in the original window display box, leading car has dummy coupling missing, otherwise complete, box is torn to one end, model appears mint. Sold for £100, Lacy, Scott & Knight, June.

Wrenn W2212 4-6-2 A4 loco and tender, 'Sir Nigel Gresley' No. 7 LNER blue, mint. Sold for £85, Lacy, Scott & Knight, June.

Wrenn W2246 2-6-4 tank loco, 'CR' blue, mint, no packer number, with instructions. Sold for £150, Lacy, Scott & Knight, June.

Wrenn 1987 50th Anniversary Limited Edition LMS maroon 6223 Princess Alice 4-6-2 locomotive and tender No. W2401, excellent in excellent box with Packer No. 3 and ref. 61147 stamped to underside, packing pieces, Limited Edition certificate No.069 and instructions. Sold for £420, Warwick and Warwick, July.

Wrenn LMS black 6256 William A Stanier FRS Duchess 8P Class 4-6-2 locomotive and tender No. W2227/A, excellent in excellent box with packing pieces. Sold for £270, Warwick and Warwick, July.

Wrenn BR maroon 46238 City of Carlisle Duchess 8P Class 4-6-2 locomotive and tender No. W2226/A, excellent in excellent reproduction box. Sold for £100, Warwick and Warwick, July.

Wrenn LNER green 4495 Great Snipe Class A4 4-6-2 locomotive and tender No. W2209/A, excellent in excellent box with Packer No. 6 to bottom of box, packing pieces and instructions. Sold for £210, Warwick and Warwick, July.

Wrenn Brighton Belle brown/ cream Car No. 90 Motor Coach No. W3006/7, generally mint in excellent box, with Packer No. 2 and ref. 441192 stamped to underside and packing pieces. Sold for £120, Warwick and Warwick, July.

Hornby Dublo BR 34042 Dorchester 3-rail locomotive and tender No.3235, good plus in good plus box, with instructions. Sold for £170, Warwick and Warwick, July.

Hornby Dublo Suburban Electric Train set No.2050, excellent in good plus box, includes S65326 and S77511 2-Car unit, track and instructions. Sold for £220, Warwick and Warwick, July.

Bachmann Virgin Trains Doctor Who Class 221 5 Car DMU Set No 32627 nearly mint to mint in good plus box. Sold for £140, Warwick and Warwick, July.

Bachmann (USA) HO/OO gauge Harry Potter and the Chamber of Secrets train set No. 00646 excellent in excellent box, with Hogwarts Railways maroon 5972 Hogwarts Castle 4-6-0 locomotive, tender, coaches (3), etc. Contents appear complete but unchecked. Sold for £95, Warwick and Warwick, July.

Bachmann DMU range with Cross Country silver 4 Car Class 220 No 32603 BR blue/grey 3 Car Class 108 No 32910 and BR green 2 Car Class 105 No 31326A mainly nearly excellent to mint. Sold for £300, Warwick and Warwick, July.

Introduction to...

Toy Figures

Vintage toy soldiers are one of the areas of collecting that blur the boundary between 'toy' and 'antique'. The very early examples made by William Britains regularly crop up on likes of *Flog It!* or even the *Antiques Roadshow*, with price tags that would raise the heart rate of most collectors!

However, although some toy figures may soar into the thousands, there are plenty of options out there to match a range of budgets - ensuring that toy soldier collecting is just as popular now as it was 120 years ago when famous British manufacturer Britains began producing lead soldiers.

William Britains is certainly a good place to start, as across the next few pages you'll see numerous examples from

Britains. Arguably it is the most popular and readily available producer of vintage toy soldiers in the UK and not a month goes by without at least a handful turning up at auction.

Like so many of its peers, Britains began by producing lead soldiers and these early pieces are the ones that venture into antique territory. This is perhaps due to the fact that, like older diecast models, they were built to be played with and classic examples are often spoilt by flaking paint, chips or missing weapons, which will all affect the value at auction. As with all collectables, the top prices are primarily achieved for those in top notch condition. Perhaps due to the fact that lead soldiers were so easily damaged, in the 1950s toy soldier manufacturers began to experiment with 'indestructable' plastic figures

and in the following decades, the market was flooded by brightly coloured soldiers, medieval knights and even cowboys.

Traditionally plastic figures are much cheaper than their lead counterparts but when it comes to rare items, both varieties can command exceptionally high prices - particularly if they're pre-production samples in unusual colours.

Along with Britains, other top toy figure names to look out for include: Barclay, Herald, Elastolin, Johillco, Lineol, Marx and Timpo. In some ways, toy figures are slightly unusual in the world of collecting because they're popular the world over, with collectors in many different countries competing to pick up scarce examples at auction.

Like model railways, toy figures also come in different scales. Britains produces models

in 1/32 scale (54mm), while others choose 1/35 (50mm) or 1/28 (60mm).

Another aspect to note is that toy figures come both unpainted and painted. Sometimes they have been painted by the manufacturer or the original owner may have painted them. Depending on the quality of the finish, this will obviously affect the final value, although a very well painted figure from an individual can still be extremely sought after.

If you're interested in collecting toy soldiers, then you're in luck because there are numerous shows dedicated to figures. The Plastic Warrior Show, held in London each year, is the oldest established show in the UK, after being founded in 1985. Events are a fantastic way to expand your knowledge about the market by sharing information with other collectors. ■

Britains set 191, Turcos in original Whisstock box, condition very good, one ankle broken, box fair, two edges of lid split, 1937. Sold for £130, C&T Auctioneers, December.

Britains RARE set 789A, British Infantry and Cavalry second grade, twenty-four Infantry and eight Cavalry in original four row Whisstock display box. Condition excellent, box good, 1937. Sold for £120, C&T Auctioneers, December.

Britains set 286, USA Cavalry at the walk and at the gallop, condition good, one fair, one horse leg missing, three horse legs repaired, box poor, 1937. Sold for £110, C&T Auctioneers, December.

Britains set 1339, Royal Horse Artillery, service dress limber and gun dark green finish, with six horse team, four mounted Gunners and Officer in khaki with peak caps, condition good, officer fair, wire traces for limber missing, officer and one trooper one horse leg repaired, one team horse leg broken and one team horse leg bent, box poor 1938. Sold for £260, C&T Auctioneers, December.

Britains set 1727, Mobile Howitzer Unit 4.5" Howitzer with Limber, Caterpillar Tender, metal tracks, khaki finish, and driver in original illustrated box. Condition good, tailgate missing, chassis damaged, one side of caterpillar loose, tyres replaced, limber towing bar broken, box poor, 1940. Sold for £65, C&T Auctioneers, December.

Britains set 1621, 12th Frontier Force at the slope in original Armies of the World box. Condition very good, one legs broken, box poor, 1938. Sold for £85, C&T Auctioneers, December.

Britains set 1885, extremely rare uncatalogued Soldiers in Action in Gasmasks not listed in catalogue, three digging and four crawling (Wallis A, 2nd Edition page 530) in original box with Soldiers in Action illustrated label. Condition very good, box fair, 1940. Sold for £150, C&T Auctioneers, December.

Britains Soldiers in Action in Gasmasks with Officer, four Crawling, five Bombers and six Charging in unusual original orange/brown box and insert card with unusual pattern of holes, possibly set 1615. Condition good, one bayonet missing, box poor, end label missing, 1940. Sold for £65, C&T Auctioneers, December.

Britains set 1343, Royal Horse Guards in Winter Cloaks with Officer, in original box. Condition very good, officer lightly embellished in gold, box poor, 1938. Two Generals and a dismounted 11th Hussar with horse. Condition excellent. Sold for £120, C&T Auctioneers, December.

Britains set 190, Belgian Cavalry at the halt, with officer in original Whisstock box. Condition very good, officer lightly embellished in gold, box fair, two splits in lid, 1939. Sold for £80, C&T Auctioneers, December.

Britains set 190, Belgian Cavalry at the halt, with Officer in original Whisstock box. Condition very good, officer lightly embellished in gold, box poor, 1939. Sold for £75, C&T Auctioneers, December.

Britains set 133, Russian Infantry at the trail with Officer, (sword bent) in original Armies of the World box with unusual end label 'U.S.S.R. Infantry'. Condition excellent, box good to fair, 1940. Sold for £130, C&T Auctioneers, December.

Britains set 110, Devonshire Regiment at the trail in original Whisstock box. Condition very good, box good, 1940. Sold for £90, C&T Auctioneers, December.

Britains set 1854, Militia shoulder arms, with early officer in khaki cap in original Battledress box. Condition excellent, box good, 1940. Sold for £100, C&T Auctioneers, December.

Britains set 1854, Militia shoulder arms, with Officer with red cap top (arm replaced) in original Battledress box. Condition excellent, box good, one end of lid split, 1940. Sold for £75, C&T Auctioneers, December.

Andrea: Black Hawk, Wild West Concord Stage Coach with six horse team, Driver, Guard and three Passengers, 1/32 scale, on dioramic stand in original box. Condition excellent, one tiny corner of roof damaged, box excellent. Sold for £160, C&T Auctioneers, April.

CBG Mignot set 275, Mounted Bugle Band of the Garde Republicaine Band Leader, with bugle, six Buglers, two Kettle Drummers (foot reins damaged) three circular horns and two trees in original wooden box with Paris background. Condition excellent, box excellent, lid slightly warped. Sold for £120, C&T Auctioneers, April.

CBG Mignot Defence de Drapeau (Defending the Colour) 1st Empire, in original dioramic scenic box. Condition excellent, box excellent, 1990. Sold for £80, C&T Auctioneers, April.

Britains sets 128F Fordson Tractor, rubber tyres with driver, in original box and 129F Timber Trailer with log. Condition very good, three log retaining pins missing, box good, 1950. Sold for £110, C&T Auctioneers, April.

Lesney Moko diecast horsedrawn Milk Float, with horse, seated milkman and five milk crates. Condition good-fair. Sold for £90, C&T Auctioneers, April.

Britains Farm card backgounds, Thatched Farmhouse and yard with Farm with passing road 73cm long approx. Card split in half, Farmhouse with yard and grass paddock with paths and cottage 82cm long approx, cottage with barn and stream 44.5cm long approx. Condition good-fair. Sold for £220, C&T Auctioneers, April.

Britains 61009 Red Lion Inn Façade, with lamp and sign, original box and outer, King and Country SP17 Normandy battle damaged Farm House with base and SP18 Farm Courtyard (five pieces, one gate spike missing) in original boxes, and Marlborough C7 Blacksmith's Shop with interior. Condition excellent. Sold for £380, C&T Auctioneers, April.

King and Country Eighth Army: EA026 Pipes and Drums of the Black Watch in original box. Condition excellent, box very good. Sold for £130, C&T Auctioneers, April.

CBG Mignot Stag Hunt, eight mounted and two dismounted Huntsmen, Huntswoman, sixteen hounds, stag, cottage, two woodstacks, two mounds of stones, ten trees and ten shrubs in box. Excellent, box very good. Sold for £280, C&T Auctioneers, April.

Dinky Toys Miniature Figures for Model Railways 'O' Gauge No 1 Station Staff, porter, ticket collector, guard and porter with luggage in dark blue uniform, engine driver in mid-blue. Very good in good box. Sold for £40, C&T Auctioneers, June.

Britains set 8, 4th Hussars, with Trumpeter, 2nd version, one-eared horses dated 1.1.1901. Condition fair, three plumes missing, two horses dented. Set 83, Middlesex Yeomanry, 2nd version cantering horses dated 12.2.1903 with Officer. Condition fair. Sold for £70, C&T Auctioneers, July.

Britains set 83, Middlesex Yeomanrywith Officer, in original Whisstock box. Condition fair, one carbine and capline missing, box fair, insert card missing, one split in side of lid, 1914. Sold for £90, C&T Auctioneers, July.

Britains set 171, Greek Infantry with Officer, Pigeon chested, no embossing on bases, in original printers type box. Condition fair, officer arm missing, box poor, 1913. Sold for £170, C&T Auctioneers, July.

Britains set 172, Bulgarian Infantry with Officer, 1st version, dated 16.1.1904 in original printers type box. Condition fair-poor, splash of red paint on officer's cap, box poor, 1913. Sold for £110, C&T Auctioneers, July.

Britains set 2018, Danish Guard Hussar Regiment, with Officer and Trumpeter in original ROAN box. Condition excellent, box good, one corner of lid split, 1954. Sold for £200, C&T Auctioneers, July.

Britains set 28, Mountain Artillery, with mounted Officer, four Mules, Gun, ammunition and six Men in original ROAN box. Condition excellent, ammunition rusty, box very good, 1956. Sold for £90, C&T Auctioneers, July.

Britains set 2025, Cameron Highlanders firing, foreign service order, six standing, three kneeling, six lying, kneeling officer, standing officer and piper in original ROAN box. Condition excellent, box fair, two corners of lid split, 1952. Sold for £130, C&T Auctioneers, July.

Britains set 200, Motor Cycle Corps Despatch Riders, in original Whisstock box. Condition very good, box fair, one corner of box split. Sold for £130, C&T Auctioneers, July.

Britains set 68, 2nd Bombay Native Infantry with Officer and Pioneer, condition good, some chips to gaiters, one gaiter retouched, 1903. Sold for £260, C&T Auctioneers, July.

Britains set 110, Devonshire Regiment, 2nd version, oval bases, Slade Wallace equipment, helmet with pugaree. Condition good, 1904. Sold for £190, C&T Auctioneers, July.

Britains set 1545, Australian Infantry, at present with Officer. Condition good, five bayonets replaced, 1938. Sold for £100, C&T Auctioneers, July.

A Crescent Toys modern farm equipment No. 1805 tractor and driver, comprising blue and red body with black rubber tyres and woman farm hand figure, housed in the original pictorial topped card box, model has little fatigue, overall near mint. Sold for £250, Lacy, Scott & Knight, August.

A Crescent Toys builders' and decorators cart set, comprising cart, ladder, bucket, tools with decorator figure, loose examples, hard to find. Sold for £15, Lacy, Scott & Knight, August.

A Britains set No. 28 Mountain Gun of the Royal Artillery, circa 1965 set, comprising 14 examples to include mounted and standing figures with four various donkeys and a gun load, loose examples, very good condition. Sold for £60, Lacy, Scott & Knight, August.

A Britains set No. 2150 Centurion tank, comprising tank finished in dark gloss green with sprung elevated turret, all four rollers apparent to underside with silver detailed tracks, very good. Sold for £65, Lacy, Scott & Knight, August.

A HM models of Great Britain white metal and hand-painted model of a Milk-Oh Express Dairies milk float circa 1890, full set limited edition No. 77/350 released, in the original foam packed box. Sold for £70, Lacy, Scott & Knight, August.

A HM Models of Great Britain white metal and handpainted gift set titled Cabby, comprising horsedrawn black painted taxi with driver figure, housed in the original buff coloured labelled box. Sold for £55, Lacy, Scott & Knight, August.

A Gainsborough Miniatures white metal 1/32 scale model of a Chores for Horses Series Milk Cart, housed in the associated blue labelled buff coloured box. Sold for £25, Lacy, Scott & Knight, August.

A Coleman's Cheshire Volunteer quality toy soldiers set titled The Farrier, white metal example housed in the original labelled box. Sold for £55, Lacy, Scott & Knight, August.

A Britains Home Farm Series No.8F Horserake, comprising a blue body with brown horse and driver figure, housed in the original green ground labelled box. Sold for £35, Lacy, Scott & Knight, August.

A Britains No.1470 The State Coach of England, housed in the original historical series, red ground labelled box, appears complete with bag of traces. Box is heavily worn. Sold for £50, Lacy, Scott & Knight, August.

A Taylor & Barrett horse-drawn brewers bray, comprising brown wagon with various beer barrel load, rear ladder and replica advertising sign. Interesting example. Sold for £80, Lacy, Scott & Knight, August.

A Herald Series from set no. H529 Antarctic Explorers, comprising sledge with 5 team husky dog unit, driver with whip and a polar skier. A loose example that would benefit from cleaning. Sold for £100, Lacy, Scott & Knight, August.

A Charbens Series travelling zoo gift set, comprising elephant-drawn cage group fitted with red bases and wheels, with base metal cages and yellow roofs, housed in the original green and white line-drawn labelled card box, some fatigue but a rare example. Sold for £150, Lacy, Scott & Knight, August.

Britains post WW2 boxed No. 901 Indian Elephant, in fine condition. Sold for £60, Special Auction Services, August.

Britains post WW2 version boxed 25Z Elephant Ride, complete with walking keeper, seat and 2 children, very good. Sold for £210, Special Auction Services, August.

Britains post WW2 version unboxed 25Z Elephant Ride, complete with walking keeper, seat and 2 children, very good. Sold for £110, Special Auction Services, August.

Britains post WW2 version of boxed set 12F Timber Carriage, in flat box, very good, complete with pins to hold log in place. Sold for £110, Special Auction Services, August.

Britains post WW2 Hunt figures from 'The Meet', restrung onto original backing card consisting of Gentleman Farmer, side saddle lady in top hat, side saddle lady in bowler hat, huntsmen on brown, and grey horses, huntsman and woman on foot, and hounds 8), generally very good, (15 pcs on card). Sold for £90, Special Auction Services, August.

Britains. Motor Cycle Corps (Dispatch Riders) Set No 200, with 4 dispatch riders on motor cycles, mis-matched figures with minor colour variation, generally good in nearly fair box, with green Whisstock label. Sold for £95, Warwick and Warwick, September.

Britains. Fort Toys West Surrey Regiment Set No 721a, with 12 soldiers marching with rifles at the slope, generally good plus in nearly good box with blue Types of the British Army illustrated label and with backing card. Sold for £80, Warwick and Warwick, September.

Britains. R.A.F. Pilots and W.A.A.F. Set No 1894, with Pilots walking in full flight gear (6) and WAAFs walking (2), general fair to nearly good in nearly good box with beige Whisstock label. Sold for £160, Warwick and Warwick, September.

Britains. Life Guards Mounted Band Set No 9406, with Musical Director with baton and 11 Bandsmen, generally excellent in poor plus box, all lid edges repaired and re-attached. Sold for £80, Warwick and Warwick, September.

Britains Limited Editions Set 5184 The Lifeguards, boxed in the style of original Britain's sets with yellow label & cream card. This set only remained on sale in this format for the original year of issue. Generally mint overall, contained in a mint set box complete with original limited edition certificate. Sold for £30, Vectis, September.

Britains Limited Editions, comprising: Set 5187 The Bahamas Police Band (1987 only). Boxed in the style of original Britain's sets with yellow labels & blue insert card. This set only remained on sale in this format for the original year of issue. Near mint overall, contained in a generally near mint set box. Sold for £25, Vectis, September.

Britains Modern Issues Special Collectors Edition Series - World War 1 Range, comprising: Set 00159 bombed street scene with 2 figures & accessories. Mint overall, contained in a generally excellent (minor storage wear) Special Collectors Edition Series Box. Sold for £70, Vectis, September.

Britains Christmas Issue, 2008, comprising: "Home for the Holidays" Christmas Tree Seller with International KB Truck & Customers. Mint, contained in a mint special edition gift box. Sold for £80, Vectis, September.

Britains Modern Issues - Collectors Club Golden Jubilee Series, 2004, comprising: Set 40259 The Prime Ministers State Coach. Mint overall, contained in a mint set box. Sold for £60, Vectis, September.

Britains Modern Issues (Premier Series), comprising: Set 8925 Royal Naval Air Service Armoured Car. Mint overall, contained in a near mint Premier Series (black and gold) set box. Sold for £80, Vectis, September.

Britains Modern Issues [Premier Series], comprising: Set 8926 Thornycroft A.A. Truck with Service Detachment. Mint overall, contained in a near mint premier series (black & gold) set box. Sold for £80, Vectis, September.

Tradition of London Traditional Style Toy Soldiers Napoleonic Wars Range, comprising: Set No B2A British Royal Horse Artillery, 1812. Painted to a high standard in the traditional toy soldier style. Mint contained in a mint tradition box. Sold for £50, Vectis, September.

Tradition Toy Style Model Soldiers, Set No 705 Troops of the Napoleonic Wars Britain 95th Rifles, 1810, comprising: Officer, Sergeant, Bugler & 5 Riflemen in action. Painted to a high standard in the traditional toy soldier style. Mint contained in a mint Tradition box. Sold for £50, Vectis, September.

CBG Mignot Napoleonic Range (post war issue) Infanterie de Ligne, Wurtemberg, 1812, comprising: Officer, Eagle Bearer, 2 Drummers & 8 Infantry Marching at the Slope. Mint overall, contained (strung) in a near mint CBG "Soldats de Plomb" labelled set box. Sold for £80, Vectis, September.

CBG Mignot Napoleonic Range (post war issue) Infanterie Legere, de Hollande, 1806, comprising: Officer, Eagle Bearer, 2 Drummers & 8 Infantry Marching at the Slope. Mint overall, contained (strung) in a near mint CBG "Soldats de Plomb" labelled set box. Sold for £80, Vectis, September.

CBG Mignot Napoleonic Range (post war issue) Battalion de Neaufchatel, 1807, comprising: Officer, Eagle Bearer, Drummer & 9 Infantry at Attention. Mint overall, contained in a near mint CBG "Soldats de Plomb" labelled set box. Sold for £70, Vectis, September.

CBG Mignot Napoleonic Range (post war issue) Musique du Infanterie du Ligne, 1806, comprising: Band Master, Chapeau Chinois & 10 Bandsmen Playing Various Instrumentation. Mint overall, contained (unstrung - no insert) in a near mint CBG "Soldats de Plomb" labelled set box. Sold for £130, Vectis, September.

CBG Mignot Napoleonic Range (post war issue) Musique des Chasseurs d'Infanterie 17 eme Legere, 1809, comprising: Band Master, Chapeau Chinois & 10 Bandsmen playing various instruments. Mint overall, contained (unstrung) in a near mint CBG "Soldats de Plomb" labelled set box. Sold for £70, Vectis, September.

CBG Mignot 1001 Nuits (The Arabian Nights) Post War Issue, comprising: 40 Piece (figures & accessories) Set representing the Sultan's Palace & the telling of the 1001 Arabian Nights stories. Mint, contained in a near mint CBG Hinged Diorama set box. Superb & Scarce. Sold for £1400, Vectis, September.

Wethra - Belgium - 13th -14th Century Heraldic Knights, 4 x Mounted Knights, includes 3 x Standard Bearers. Depicted in various action poses with various weapons. Painted to a high commercial standard most figures are named to the underside of the base. Mint overall. Sold for £90, Vectis, September.

Introduction to...
Tinplate Toys

Tinplate toys are some of the most colourful and charming of all vintage collectables. What's more, the variety of subjects covered from fairly standard classic cars to whacky designs from outer space, ensures there's a huge range of themes for collectors to choose from.

Rather like toy soldiers, the earliest tinplate examples date back to the mid 19th century, as tinplate steel began to replace wood as the material of choice for children's toys. The steel could be bent into a range of shapes and decorated with colourful transfers, giving manufacturers a much wider choice of designs.

In the early days, Germany led the way in tinplate, with the likes of Lehmann, Marklin and Bing dominating the market throughout the 19th century and early 20th century - if you stumble across one of these tinplate toys at a car boot, then you've really struck it lucky.

As tinplate became more popular, other countries entered into the fray, with Louis Marx in America producing a huge selection of tinplate until the middle of the 20th century.

Unfortunately World War I and II had a huge effect on tinplate production, as steel was required for the war effort, instead of making toys. As such, finding pieces produced around these periods is extremely tough. After the war was over, German tinplate was produced within the 'US Zones' and are often stamped with this description. The US Zone only applied from 1945 to 1949, making it much easier to date examples from this period.

After World War II a new player entered the market: Japan. The idea was that the country would produce cheap tinplate toys that could be sold in America. Japan excelled in tinplate production, making some incredibly detailed toys with innovative clockwork or battery-operated functions. What's more, as America and the USSR entered into the space race during the 1950s, Japan was quick to capitalise on the sudden popularity of space travel, releasing a plethora of colourful spaceships and alien robots. Some of the best were produced by the likes of Horikawa and Yonezawa. Now, most modern tinplate toys tend to be produced

in China - again, noting the country of manufacture will help you date any tinplate you've acquired.

Tinplate toys are especially popular in America and US auction houses - such as Morphy's Auctions and Bertoia - often achieve some of the best prices for vintage tinplate, particularly those produced in America and Japan. Over in the UK, Marklin and Lehmann models often take the top spots, with some exchanging hands for six-figure sums.

Unfortunately, due to the fact they're made from metal, rust poses a large problem for tinplate. Although most collectors will accept a spot or two of rust - especially if the model is an older example - the best prices are achieved by those in mint condition. Also, boxes are hugely important, especially those colorful examples from the '50s and '60s depicting fantastic images of space travel.

Sadly in the 1960s, just as tinplate had replaced wood, plastic replaced tinplate bringing an end to the golden era of terrific tinplate toys. ∎

Bandai (Japan) 705 Austin Healey 100/Six Convertible, scarce variation with open top is metallic blue with tinprinted interior, friction drive - excellent plus and comes in a good card box with correct illustration to lid, 8"/21cm long. Sold for £130, December, Vectis.

Bandai (Japan) "Stock Car Series" tinplate friction drive Austin Healey, scarce example is red with white side panels, black roof with tinprinted interior detail, checker effect to rear boot, racing number 8 to roof and sides with Austin Healey Script to bonnet, the mechanism is worn but bodily the model is excellent plus, 8"/21cm long and comes in a scarce window box for this series. Sold for £80, December, Vectis.

Bandai (Japan) "Race Car Series" tinplate Austin Healey in competition finish, two-tone orangey red/white with tinprinted blue interior, racing number 8 to bonnet and sides with Austin Healey Script to rear. Excellent plus, 8"/21cm long and comes in a good plus window box. Sold for £90, December, Vectis.

Bandai (Japan) tinplate friction drive Austin Healey, 8"/21cm model is metallic red, with tinprinted brown interior and blue dashboard, friction drive in working order - excellent plus. Sold for £70, December, Vectis.

Joustra (France) tinplate friction drive "Austin Healey Cabriolet", scarce early example is red, with tinprinted interior detail, black roof, racing number 3, early version has opening bonnet to reveal engine detail, fitted with white plastic hubs and rubber tyres, 21cm/8" long. Good plus and comes in a good card box. Sold for £70, December, Vectis.

Joustra (France) Austin Healey hard top, cream, with tinprinted detail to interior, racing number 3 to sides, this version with detailed tinplate hub caps, may benefit from further cleaning - otherwise generally excellent, 8"/21cm long. Sold for £45, December, Vectis.

Joustra (France) "Remote Control Austin Healey", rare example is red, 8.5"/21cm long, black roof with tinprinted interior detail, chrome hubs, steerable front wheels and brake to rear, the motor is in working order and comes with a key, the mechanical steering control is attached to the rear. Excellent plus scarce toy which comes in a good plus illustrated box. Sold for £80, December, Vectis.

Joustra (France) tinplate Austin Healey Convertible, later free-wheeling model is dark blue, with racing number 11 to bonnet, tinprinted interior. Excellent plus, 8"/20cm long. Sold for £90, December, Vectis.

Joustra (France) tinplate clockwork remote control Austin Healey, early example with opening bonnet to reveal engine detail, finished in red with black roof and tinprinted interior detail, racing number 3, not fitted with key but the motor is in working order with brake and untested mechanical remote steering control attached, 8"/21cm long. Some age related wear otherwise good plus. Sold for £45, December, Vectis.

Joustra (France) tinplate free-wheeling Austin Healey, light green, tinprinted interior detail, with tinplate spoked wheels, racing number 11. Excellent, includes clear plastic windscreen. Sold for £45, December, Vectis.

Tri-ang Minic 1/20th scale electric Austin Healey Opentop Convertible, red plastic body, cream interior, fitted with after market racing number 5 stickers and cream infill panel behind front bumper - otherwise good plus to excellent. Unusually this model comes in a good Harlequin pattern card box. Sold for £90, December, Vectis.

Tri-ang Minic 1/20th scale Austin Healey 100/Six Opentop Convertible, metallic grey plastic body with cream interior and infill panel behind front bumper, the original windscreen requires reattachment but is present. Excellent plus and comes in a good illustrated box with inner card display base. Sold for £110, December, Vectis.

Tri-ang Minic electric Austin Healey 100/Six Opentop Convertible, dark red with cream interior, the original windscreen requires refitting but is present - otherwise the car is excellent plus and comes in a good plus illustrated box with inner card display base and foldout 4-sided colour catalogue. Sold for £120, December, Vectis.

Tri-ang Minic 1/20th scale Austin Healey Convertible Opento, 1/20th scale electric model with metallic grey plastic body and cream interior, windscreen intact. Near mint in a good illustrated box with inner card display base and 4-sided instruction book showing contemporary range. Sold for £150, December, Vectis.

Startex tinplate clockwork Austin Healey, 1/32nd scale in scarce two-tone metallic blue/cream finish. Composition driver, clockwork pull-cord to rear is present, light wear to the drivers door otherwise good plus to excellent. Sold for £260, December, Vectis.

Schuco Varianto Cabriolet 3045, tinplate clockwork car resembling an Austin Healey in beige, clockwork motor in working order and comes with a key - excellent. Sold for £80, December, Vectis.

Tri-ang large Circus Van, in blue and red in played with condition, needs cleaning, fair. Sold for £50, Lacy, Scott & Knight, April.

An Arnold tinplate and mechanical Primal Saloon comprising of maroon body with white wall tyres, driver and passenger figures, with working hand control, loose example. Sold for £100, Lacy, Scott & Knight, April.

A Corgi Toys Mettoy re-issue tin plate and clockwork limited edition London Transport bus, fitted with clockwork mechanism and housed in the original re-released box. Sold for £20, Lacy, Scott & Knight, April.

A Schuco No. 763 Cytra Ambassador 38 yacht comprising of plastic white and red hull with Schuco lettering, complete with brown and white superstructure, housed in the remains of the polystyrene packaging with power unit. Sold for £30, Lacy, Scott & Knight, April.

A Schuco No. 351226 Elektro BMW turbo race car, comprising of orange body with a removable battery box and handset, housed in the original polystyrene packaging. Sold for £20, Lacy, Scott & Knight, April.

Tri-ang Minic Articulated Transport Lorry, coupling requires re-asembling but all parts present. In very good condition but with marks to roof of cab, very good, box good. Sold for £120, Lacy, Scott & Knight, April.

Arnold of West Germany, 87001 (re-issue) tinplate steamer boat, mint in box. Sold for £50, Lacy, Scott & Knight, April.

Taiyo Tinplate battery powered Ford Mustang, tiny rub mark to roof, very near mint in box. Sold for £90, Lacy, Scott & Knight, April.

Early 20th Century Tinplate Penny-Toy train, LMS, play worn in fair condition for its age. Sold for £65, Lacy, Scott & Knight, April.

Paramount Electrical Toys, 3 piece Miniature Flood Light, Petrol Pump and Light House set, in the original box, with repaired lid. Sold for £60, Lacy, Scott & Knight, April.

A boxed "Cyro Cycle" by Tri-ang, complete with card insert, cycle in very good to near mint condition, box complete but is a bit tired. Near mint, good box. Sold for £110, Lacy, Scott & Knight, April.

A Gunthermann tinplate clockwork continental holiday touring coach, complete with key in very good condition for age. Sold for £70, Lacy, Scott & Knight, April.

A Schuco vintage tinplate clockwork car in a garage "Kommando Anno 2000" circa mid 40s complete with original key. Good. Sold for £60, Lacy, Scott & Knight, April.

A Shackleton Models FG6 tipper comprising of blue to grey and scarlet red body, fitted with clockwork motor and bearing the Shackleton Toys emblem to inside of trailer, model petrol tanks have been overpainted, housed in the original Foden FG6 tipper, all card box, mechanism is in working order. Sold for £340, Lacy, Scott & Knight, April.

A Shackleton Toys clockwork model of a Foden FG flat bed truck, comprising dark blue cab and back with grey chassis and red mudguards, fitted with silver hubs and housed in the original heavily worn all-card box, with key and wrench, and a reproduction instruction leaflet. Very good, box good. Sold for £260, Lacy, Scott & Knight, April.

A Shackleton Toys model of a Foden FG flatbed lorry, comprising dark blue cab and back with red mudguards and grey chassis, petrol tanks have been over painted, housed in a replacement all-card box. Very good. Sold for £200, Lacy, Scott & Knight, April.

A Shackleton Models model of a Foden FG6 tipper truck, comprising two-tone blue body with repainted mudguards and petrol tanks fitted with grey chassis and housed in a reproduction all-card box. Sold for £220, Lacy, Scott & Knight, April.

Tri-ang Spot-on 404 (N104) Morris Mini Van, yellow body, cream interior, silver trim and chrome hubs with "Ferodo" labels to van sides - promotional model. Small label peel to nearside otherwise near mint unboxed. Sold for £320, Vectis, April.

Tri-ang Minic "Minic Brewery" Forward Control Lorry with Articulated Trailer, green cab with red rear body, includes load of 8 x wooden barrels and a key, the motor is in working order - generally good in a fair card box. Sold for £140, Vectis, April.

Tri-ang Minic 30M Mechanical Horse and Pantechnicon Trailer, scarce tinplate clockwork model from the 1950s, unusual to find "Carter Paterson and Pickfords Joint Parcels Services" to the green trailer, which also has its opening rear doors and locking door. The prime move has a red standard cab, some deterioration to the rubber tyres, no key but the clockwork motor is in working order, some age related wear but overall a good plus to excellent. Sold for £200, Vectis, April.

Tri-ang Minic Dust Cart, dark blue standard cab with red rear body, bright plated parts, slight corrosion to the front wing near the keyhole, no key, the motor is in working order, slight paint loss near keyhole area otherwise an excellent bright example which comes in a fair card box Sold for £70, Vectis, April.

Tri-ang Minic Pre-War Rolls Royce Sedanca 50ME, with electric lights. Scarce model is two-tone green with green hood, black plastic seats, opening rear boot to reveal battery compartment and wire, 2 x bulbs to front headlamps. Lacks its key but the motor is in working order, generally good plus to excellent. Sold for £360, Vectis, April.

Tri-ang Minic 1/20th scale Hillman Minx electric model Car scarce example finished in sage green with cream interior, bright plated parts, clean battery compartment to underside, excellent. Sold for £110, Vectis, April.

Yonezawa (Japan) Lincoln XL-500 tinplate "Concept Car" futuristic model is red, with clear plastic roof, detailed tinprinted interior, some slight surface corrosion to the plated parts - otherwise a good. Sold for £220, Vectis, April.

JNF Favorit large tinplate Open Top Car, lime green with red interior, tinprinted dashboard, the motor is in working order and comes with a key, steerable front wheels, circa 1950s. Excellent in a poor box. Sold for £120, Vectis, April.

Arnold (Germany) 2800 "Primat" tinplate remote control Car with tinprinted interior, male driver and female passenger, cable attached to rear with mechanical remote control, wind-up remote control powers the vehicle forwards. Excellent in a poor box. Sold for £110, Vectis, April.

Joustra (France) large tinplate Ford "Pick-up Truck with Camera" clockwork mechanism, no key but the motor is in working order. Finished in orange with light blue roof and tinprinted interior detail, bright plated parts Sold for £140, Vectis, April.

Ichiko Chevrolet Impala Police Car, friction drive tinplate car circa 1960s. Black/white Police livery, detailed tinprinted interior, friction drive in working order with oscillating roof beacons together with aerial, otherwise good plus. Sold for £60, Vectis, June.

Tri-ang Minic 22M "ATCO Lawn Mowers" Promotional Van circa 1950s, scarce example with mid-green standard cab, red rear van body, some surface corrosion coming through on the wings and age related marks, lacks rear locking bar motor is in working order - fair. Sold for £45, Vectis, June.

Tipp & Co (Tippco Germany) tinplate clockwork Mercedes Unimog Breakdown Truck. Scarce item is orange, with red jib, tinprinted cab detail, no key but clockwork motor is in working order with brake lever in the cab, tilting clear plastic windscreen with tan coloured plastic roof attached, steerable front wheels, some scratching to the roof otherwise good plus example becoming harder to find. Sold for £80, Vectis, June.

Kenton/Arcade cast iron Mack 6-wheeled Lorry Mounted Crane with Shovel Loader attachment. Circa 1920s scarce American toy with wooden hubs and white rubber tyres, some overall play wear including the rubber tyres but generally a good unusual example which has survived very well. Sold for £80, Vectis, June.

Marklin 1102 tinplate clockwork Mercedes Sports Car. Of recent limited edition production, this tinplate model is finished in silver with red seat, racing number 4, steerable front wheels, includes a key, with "Karl Kling" signature to bonnet. Mint in an excellent card box with inner packaging and certificate. Sold for £70, Vectis, June.

Tri-ang Minic "Mechanical Horse and Cable Trailer". Articulated Lorry with red standard cab, mid-green Low Loader Trailer with 2 x grey plastic BICC containers, circa 1950's with cast metal hubs, no key but the motor is in working order, slight spidering to the roof otherwise good plus to excellent and comes in a fair illustrated card box. Sold for £100, Vectis, June.

Mettoy 1940s large tinplate clockwork articulated lorry, dark green with tinprinted detail including 8 x balloon wheels, clockwork motor requires attention, lacks front mudguards otherwise fair. Sold for £25, Vectis, June.

Tippco (Tipp & Co of Germany) "Express" Delivery Van, scarce tinplate friction drive example circa 1960 is dark green/cream with opening rear door and locking catch - an excellent plus bright example. Sold for £80, Vectis, June.

Tri-ang Minic mid 1950s tinplate clockwork Double Decker Bus, one of the last of clockwork versions, fitted with red plastic hubs, pedal motors and Bovril adverts, no key but the motor is in working order, some light play wear but overall a good to good plus bright example. Sold for £120, Vectis, June.

Wells (UK) Mickey Mouse tinplate clockwork hand operated Railway Truck, designed to run on O Gauge track, detailed tinprinting with substantial clockwork motor, comes with painted plaster figures with metal hands of Mickey Mouse and Donald Duck, some repairs to Mickey's ankles and faint cracks above Donald's feet. Otherwise a good example with no key but with clockwork motor in working order. Sold for £140, Vectis, July.

Arnold (US Zone of Germany) tinplate clockwork Monkey on a Tricycle, detailed tinprinting, no key but the novelty figure has a pedalling action as the tricycle is propelled forward and the monkey periodically turns the handlebars. Just light age related wear - otherwise a good plus. Sold for £80, Vectis, July.

Schuco (Germany) Curvo 1000 tinplate clockwork Motorcycle red/cream with rider wearing shirt and brown pants, detailed tinprinting, no key but the motor is in working order. Light age wear otherwise generally excellent for display. Sold for £100, Vectis, July.

Technofix (Germany) tinplate clockwork Motorcycle with registration number GE258 red, with grey/cream tinprinted detail, rider wearing grey trousers and beige shirt, racing number 4 to his back, clockwork motor with integral key in working orders, light surface rust to the small stabiliser wheel at the rear on the right hand side. Excellent plus and comes with the remains of a instruction slip. Sold for £70, Vectis, July.

Tipp & Co (Tippco of Germany) large friction drive tinplate Police Motorcycle circa 1950s. Green/cream tinprinting, some age related wear here and there, a small hole has been drilled in the top of the petrol tank and lacks the clear plastic windscreen. Good plus with friction drive still in working order. Sold for £160, Vectis, July.

Technofix (Germany) 202 friction drive Scooter with Rider and Lady Passenger, friction drive in working order, tinplate model with colourful tinprinting, lacks the windscreen but does include the rear spare wheel, otherwise good plus. Sold for £70, Vectis, July.

Sutcliffe Models (UK) "The Bluebird Wonder Speedboat" clockwork model blue hull, white deck and orange fittings, the motor requires attention but does include the propeller and rudder for display and comes in a fair card box. Sold for £50, Vectis, July.

Sutcliffe Models "Nautilus" Submarine from Walt Disney's 20 Leagues Under the Sea by Jules Verne, tinplate clockwork model is green, some nicks and scratches but the motor is in working order with a plain key. Good including illustrated box with inner packing piece. Sold for £100, Vectis, July.

Bandai (Japan) "Cadillac with Dashboard", large scale tinplate battery operated Cadillac as a 2-door Coupe, finished in metallic gold with tinprinted interior and hub caps, remote control cable attached with tinplate dashboard style control unit, untested but with a clean battery compartment includes steering wheel and gear shift handle, some nicks and scratches to the car and lacks a wing mirror. Generally good, in fair illustrated box. Sold for £260, Vectis, July.

Lehmann (Germany) 688 "Mensa" tinplate clockwork 3-wheeled Table Top Delivery Van with Rod, early version circa late 1920's with driver figure, some surface corrosion and age related wear, the clockwork motor is present but the spring requires attention but does include the opening rear compartment door and locking catch. Fair. Sold for £180, Vectis, July.

Mettoy (UK) tinplate clockwork AA Motorcycle Patrol dark blue bike with tinprinting, yellow uniformed rider and petrol tank, clockwork motor in working order with stabiliser wheels. Generally good overall. Sold for £150, Vectis, July.

Roy Cox (Thimble Drone Champion) aluminium Tether Racing Car red, with blue baseplate, racing number 99, includes part of a glow plug type motor to interior, unchecked for completeness with some wear particularly to the rear end - otherwise generally good. Sold for £110, Vectis, July.

Meccano Constructor Aeroplane, built as a Biplane, red, with silver wings, blue struts and propeller, fitted with 2 floats and RAF roundels, some age related wear, dating from the 1930s - otherwise fair to good. Sold for £80, Vectis, July.

Meccano Constructor Aeroplane - constructed as a Biplane, with cream fuselage and red wings, RAF roundels, this model fitted with 2 x wheels to the undercarriage, when propelled forward on its wheels the propeller revolves, some age related wear but overall fair to good for display. Sold for £120, Vectis, July.

Kenton (USA) or similar cast iron 2-wheeled Coal Cart circa 1930s, red cart with shafts, 2 yellow spoked wheels with cast iron horse and driver and reins - fair to good scarce example. Sold for £60, Vectis, July.

Marx Toys (USA) 1940s tinplate Tank, green, with tinprinted detail, fitted with substantial clockwork motor and integral key, drives the vehicle forward with clicking action, includes both rubber tracks and fitted with a working brake. Excellent example. Sold for £60, Vectis, July.

Bandai (Japan) tinplate Lincoln Continental, red, with tinprinted interior detail and hub caps, friction drive in working order to rear wheels and includes the clear plastic windscreen, some light play wear to some of the edges and discreet retouching to a repair to the drivers side rear fin - otherwise good for display. Sold for £70, Vectis, July.

Gama (Germany) friction drive Opel Kapitan 4-door Saloon, 1950s tinplate friction drive example is metallic blue with matching off-white roof, detailed tinprinted interior, included whitewall tyres with all 4 hub caps, some age related wear but does include the Opel plastic bonnet logo and Kapitan printing to both front wings together with steerable front wheels - otherwise a good scarce example. Sold for £120, Vectis, July.

CK Toys (Kuramochi of Japan) tinplate clockwork "Streamline Highspeed Passenger Train", scarce example of a clockwork Railcar, no key but the motor is in working order, fitted with 6 x wheels to underside, silver in colour with red/yellow printing to sides, possibly a pre-war example - good plus for display. Sold for £100, Vectis, July.

Alps (Japan) "Mercedes Benz 230SL Kabrio" battery operated tinplate sports car is red, with tinprinted detail including hub caps, some slight rippling effect to the bonnet but does include the plastic driver figure, steerable front wheels and a clean battery compartment. Good in a good plus illustrated box. Sold for £160, Vectis, July.

Blomer and Schuler (Germany) tinplate clockwork Walking Peacock novelty toy dating from circa 1920s/30s with detailed tinprinting, no key but the motor is in working order producing a walking action with fanning movement to the tail. A good plus example. Sold for £150, Vectis, July.

Masudaya (Modern Toys of Japan) "Non-Stop Lavender Robot" this is an original mega rare Robot from 1959, highly prized by robot collectors from what is known as the Golden Era circa 1960s and is one of the "Gang of 5" rare robots from that period. Owned by the vendor from new, lilac in colour with tinprinted detail. The head is loose owing to lacking one of the 4 securing tabs but is lightly tacked onto the body using the other 3 for display. The robot is fitted with the on/off toggle switch to the front and a clean battery compartment to the underside, untested but fitted with mystery action wheels to the baseplate, very light age related wear and minor spidering to the vintage paint work but otherwise a good plus example for display. Sold for £1500, Vectis, July.

Tri-ang Minic 1950s tinplate Caravan, scarce item produced towards the end of production has a cream upper and red lower body, opening door, later issue black plastic wheels, includes tow hook. Excellent plus to near mint bright example which comes in a good illustrated box. Sold for £80, Vectis, July.

Tri-ang Minic 119M Watneys Barrel Lorry, dark green standard cab with wooden barrel to trailer, includes red painted diecast hubs and plastic barrel to the cab roof, would benefit from further polishing, comes with a key - otherwise good plus to excellent bright example which comes in a good plus illustrated box marked "Watney Lorry" and a fair colour foldout catalogue showing contemporary range. Sold for £170, Vectis, July.

Tri-ang Minic "Jabberwock" tinplate/plastic novelty toy circa 1950s, scarce example is blue/green, no key but in excellent working order, 8"/20cm long and comes in a fair card box which lacks an end flap. Sold for £100, Vectis, July.

Tri-ang large pressed steel Routemaster Bus circa 1960, red, 22"/56cm long, fair example. Sold for £100, Vectis, July.

Taiyo (Japan) tinplate "Screaming Siren" Police Car, tinplate battery operated large scale Ford 4-door Sedan. Excellent plus and comes in a good window box. Sold for £100, Vectis, July.

Biller Toys (US Zone of Germany) tinplate clockwork Racing Car, red/cream with racing number 7, some light age related wear - otherwise generally a good plus bright example with no key but in working order. Sold for £30, Vectis, July.

Tri-ang large pressed steel Routemaster Bus circa 1960's, has had some partial restoration to the roof and other panels with some reproduction stickers, red with white interior. Done to a fair standard. Sold for £150, Vectis, July.

Tri-ang Minic "Watney Lorry" circa 1950's with green forward control cab, trailer with large wooden barrel, red painted cast metal hubs, some light wear but in working order with correct key. Good plus in a fair to good illustrated box. Sold for £60, Vectis, July.

Tri-ang "Motor Lifeboat" white/blue, the deck fittings are unchecked for completeness but overall the boat is excellent and in working order with correct Minic key, includes rudder and brass propeller. Sold for £300, Vectis, July.

Sutcliffe Models "Valiant" tinplate clockwork Battleship, scarce example with black lower hull, grey upper hull and super structure, later issue in working order, complete with key and catalogue depicting contemporary range, rear propeller and rudder both in working order but lacks mast. All contained in excellent illustrated box. Sold for £130, Vectis, August.

Sutcliffe Models "Hawk" tinplate clockwork Speedboat, sea green, white deck, lacks rear plastic flag but motor is in working order, complete with key, rear propeller and rudder. Small scratch to front of deck otherwise good plus to excellent in fair illustrated box. Sold for £35, Vectis, August.

Sutcliffe Models "Sea Wolf" tinplate clockwork Submarine, yellow, includes rubber bung (rubber is perished), in working order and complete with key, propeller and rudder. Excellent in good illustrated box with inner packaging. Sold for £60, Vectis, August.

Sutcliffe Models "Comet" tinplate clockwork Speedboat, scarce example in powder blue, lacks key and some wear around deck area but motor is in working order, with rear propeller and rudder. Good in fair illustrated box (missing end flaps at one end). Sold for £30, Vectis, August.

Sutcliffe Models "Racer I" tinplate clockwork Speedboat, scarce earlier example with red hull, orange deck and blue engine cover, with replacement key, motor in working order together with propeller and rudder. Good to good plus. Sold for £90, Vectis, August.

Sutcliffe Models "Fury" Torpedo Boat, tinplate clockwork early example with red hull, metallic grey deck and super structure, working order and comes with Chad Valley key, propeller and rudder. Sold for £90, Vectis, August.

Hornby pre-war Speedboat "Swift", red hull and engine cover, cream deck - working order with replacement key, together with rear rudder and propeller, motor is fitted with brake. Some age related wear particularly to edges otherwise generally good in fair early card box with illustrated label to lid. Sold for £60, Vectis, August.

Victory Industries (UK) "Miss England" Super Silent Speedboat, scarce boat of aluminium construction from the immediate post-war period circa 1948, 2-piece aluminium construction, fitted with internal burner and works off hot air system. Good for display and measuring 14"/36cm long, in fair illustrated box. Sold for £180, Vectis, August.

Victory Industries (UK) "Vosper" Triple Screw Express Turbine Yacht, scarce example featuring black hull, tan/white deck and super structure, made for electric propulsion - untested, superstructure slides forward to give access to electric motor and battery compartment, unchecked for completeness. Fair in poor to fair remains of illustrated box. Sold for £45, Vectis, August.

Kellner/Lines Bros 1930s clockwork wooden Speedboat "Triang Speedboat No.4" 2922, painted cream with red/blue lining, no key but motor appears to be in working order and is fitted with brake, rudder and propeller, in original finish. These "K" wooden boats were in the 1930s Tri-ang Toys catalogue following a deal with the German manufacturer Kellner. Does have glue repair to loose engine cover otherwise overall a good example measuring 24"/61cm long and unusually still retains a fair to good card box marked "WS7CW Boat" and with Kellner label at one end. Sold for £260, Vectis, August.

Lindberg (USA) 1/125 scale "Blue Devil Destroyer" large scale kit, unchecked for completeness and appears to be a body only kit but otherwise parts are good to excellent in good illustrated box with 8-page instruction book. Sold for £45, Vectis, August.

TMY/ITO (Japan) electric powered Naval Gun Boat, light blue, red lower hull, abundance of metal fittings including guns, ventilators, levers etc. The super structure is removable to reveal the engine and battery compartment and brass control levers. There are 2 x TMY vintage electric motors fitted with horseshoe magnets driving the rear propellers (one shaft lacks propeller) together with rudder, one of the torpedo tubes is loose inside hold while the other is missing, crack in woodwork on deck area near to opening compartment. Whole ship would benefit from further cleaning otherwise fair. Sold for £240, Vectis, August.

TMY/ITO (Japan) battery operated Warship, light blue, with metal fittings to deck including guns, ventilators and electric lamps etc., one of the torpedo tubes is detached but present (in the hold), the vessel includes both propellers to rear and rudder, super structure is removable to reveal engine compartment which has only one TMY vintage electric motor with horseshoe magnet (other motor is missing) but does include brass control levers and battery compartment, removable decking area lacks piece of wooden deck in one corner. Ship is painted in light blue with red lower hull - would benefit from further cleaning and some light restoration but otherwise a fair to good scarce. Sold for £70, Vectis, August.

French made large wooden Pond Yacht,, solid wooden hull with lead weight to keel, main mast with 3 x sails - one is marked No.504, main mast stands 30"/75cm above the deck. Some light wear but overall good plus. Sold for £30, Vectis, August.

Large Seifert-Boot - German made Pond Yacht, with red and white plastic hull and keel, lever operated rudder, varnished wooden deck, some metal fittings, may lack sails to an additional mast otherwise a Good project for some restoration, 36"/91cm long. Sold for £30, Vectis, August.

Hornby pre-war tinplate Speedboat "Coronation" issue, scarce clockwork example finished in red with cream deck. This issue has applied transfer to bow celebrating the coronation in 1937 with profile portraits of King George VI and Queen Elizabeth within a laurel wreath. With non-standard key, clockwork motor is in working order driving the rear propeller and is fitted with rudder and working brake - good together with poor to fair illustrated box. Sold for £60, Vectis, August.

Bing (Germany) tinplate clockwork 3-Funnelled Liner, metallic copper coloured lower hull, black upper, white/yellow super structure, lacks lifeboat and rear flag, plus both masts have been repainted otherwise clockwork motor is in working order with key and does include rear propeller and rudder - Good overall. Sold for £170, Vectis, August.

FROG Mark IV Interceptor
FROG Mark IV Interceptor Fighter Aeroplane "With Foreign Markings", scarce example, the aluminium fuselage body is finished in US Army green, paper wings and US markings. Also includes white painted propeller, various tools, oil bottle and clockwork winding mechanism - unchecked for completeness but generally good in fair illustrated box. Sold for £60, Vectis, August.

Burnett (Chad Valley UK) "Ubilda Loco", scarce pre-war tinplate, clockwork kit for 4-4-2 Tank Locomotive. Tinprinted in green, unchecked for completeness but does come with body parts and wheels etc. together with 4-wheeled clockwork driving mechanism. Excellent, scarce example in good plus illustrated box with 8-sided catalogue depicting contemporary range. Sold for £110, Vectis, August.

Chad Valley (UK) "Ubilda Locomotive", tinplate, clockwork parts to build 4-4-2 LMS Tank Locomotive - unchecked for completeness but contents appear excellent in good plus to excellent illustrated post-war box. Sold for £110, Vectis, August.

Chad Valley (UK) "Ubilda Touring Car", kit with parts to build tinplate, clockwork 2-seater Open Top Car. Unchecked for completeness but contains 4 wheels, clockwork motor to rear axle, radiator grille, body parts, seats, running boards etc. Kit has had some use but otherwise good to good plus in good illustrated box. Sold for £200, Vectis, August.

Burnett "Ubilda Airliner", scarce pre-war kit comprising tinplate wings, fuselage and other parts, clockwork under carriage and some tools - to produce pre-war mechanically propelled airliner. Unchecked for completeness but appears good plus to excellent in good plus illustrated box and instruction sheet. Sold for £170, Vectis, August.

Sutcliffe "Chris-Craft Special Race Boat", late production tinplate clockwork produced for the Windermere Steam Boat Dock Museum, issued by Chris-Craft of Florida, USA, no key but motor is in working order, with rudder and propeller. Near mint in plain card box, with some literature. Sold for £380, Vectis, September.

CK Toys (Karamochi Toys of Japan) 1930s tinplate Submarine, scarce example finished in grey, black trim, white superstructure, fitted with gyro motor although handle is not quite engaging through wear, but does include rear flag, rudder and propeller, metal stand detached but present. Good plus for display, 13"/33cm long. Sold for £140, Vectis, September.

Hornby Speed Boats "Swift", pre-war tinplate clockwork speed boat. No key but motor is in good working order with brake, rudder and propeller, 13"/34cm long. Sold for £45, Vectis, September.

Hornby Speed Boats "Racer II", powder blue with white deck and dark blue trim, lacks part of windscreen and rubber, motor winds but spring requires attention otherwise fair. Sold for £45, Vectis, September.

Lehmann (Germany) 672 "St Vincent" tinplate clockwork Warship, grey/red, with tinprinted deck detail, some repainted deck fittings otherwise generally good, clockwork motor is in working order with integral key although motor may require lubrication, unchecked for completeness but a scarce pre-war item, 14"/35cm long. Sold for £90, Vectis, September.

TPS tinplate "Champion Stunt Car", battery operated model based on Ford Mustang, with drag racing style tinprinting, rubber tyres, untested but appears excellent plus, 11"/28cm long - in good illustrated box. Sold for £60, Vectis, September.

Mettoy (UK) 6-wheeled "Pool" Tanker, large tinplate clockwork model circa 1940s - grey, clockwork motor with integral key in working order, some play wear and repainting to back panel plus Mettoy or similar spring loaded Gun - 3-colour camouflage, fair. Sold for £120, Vectis, September.

Gunthermann or similar clockwork Car, repainted in pale metallic blue, registration number SGC 1010 to front and rear, no key but motor is in working order, otherwise overall good for display, 10.5"/26cm long. Sold for £45, Vectis, September.

Mettoy (UK) Articulated Army Lorry , large scale example finished in 2-colour camouflage, with 4-wheeled tractor unit and trailer, detailed tinprinting, includes uniformed driver figure, opening rear tailgate, with "44th Division No.128" insignia to each cab door initials "RASC" to body sides, some wear to loading deck otherwise Fair to Good example with working clockwork motor - unusual in this livery, circa 1940s. Sold for £90, Vectis, September.

Marx Toys or similar tinplate clockwork 2-door Sedan, dark green, fitted with balloon wheels, some age related wear and no key but clockwork motor is in working order, with brake, circa 1940s, 12"/30cm long. Sold for £50, Vectis, September.

Gunthermann (Bavaria) pre-war Tram Car, scarce tinplate clockwork model is green/cream, lacks the trolleypole but does include the tinplate driver at one end, brass lamp bezels at each end, the clockwork motor appears in working order but does need attention, the spoked tinplate wheels have been re-soldered onto their axles but overall a good scarce example circa 1930's. Sold for £160, Vectis, September.

Burnett (Chad Valley of England) pre-war Single Decker Bus, scarce large scale tinplate clockwork example with registration number 32554 in grey/red "Red & White" livery. A wooden replacement roof has been retro fitted and painted cream and replacement tinplate balloon wheels have been fitted, the motor has been disconnected but otherwise still a fair scarce example which could be improved. Sold for £50, Vectis, September.

Burnett (Chad Valley of England) tinplate Fordson type Tipper Lorry, a very scarce example dating from 1939. This model was first shown in the 1939 catalogue but was not continued in the same form after the war. Finished in orange, with tinprinted detail, balloon wheels, nut & bolt construction, the winding gear is complete but does require attention otherwise a good plus example. Sold for £120, Vectis, September.

Schylling "Lionel Lines" tinplate Railcar with propeller, scarce limited edition production model of recent issue, comes with a key, the rear propeller is in working order with brake. Excellent plus to near mint in excellent packaging (although some yellowing to the clear plastic cover). Designed to run on O Gauge track. Sold for £30, Vectis, September.

Mohr & Krauss "Centrimobil" tinplate Gyro powered open-top Car, green with red embossed trim, includes uniformed chauffeur figure, motor is in working order, actuated by a winding handle at the front (gearing slightly worn), some nicks & scratches but otherwise generally a good bright example for display. Sold for £60, Vectis, September.

An Eastern European tinplate Space Gun, scarce friction drive ex-shop stock example is black/pale blue with tinprinted Spaceman images, friction drive. Near mint, 10"/24cm long and comes in a good illustrated box with manufacturers instruction slip and some inner packaging. Sold for £80, Vectis, September.

DMI "Winner 93 Motorcycle", friction drive tinplate racing bike with clicking action and moveable rider, some adhesive tape marks otherwise excellent in a good plus illustrated box. Sold for £35, Vectis, September.

West German tinplate pair of spinning planes, in need of some attention. Sold for £35, Hansons Auctioneers, September.

A boxed tinplate, clockwork motorcycle, working order, in original box, damaged. Sold for £35, Hansons Auctioneers, September.

An unboxed Yonezawa vintage car, battery operated, driven by man in bowler hat. Battery box corroded. Sold for £35, Hansons Auctioneers, September.

A boxed tinplate Rosko, Bartender with Revolving Eyes, battery powered, in need of some attention but does appear to work. Sold for £30, Hansons Auctioneers, September.

An unboxed Nomura Mystery Police Car, battery operated, in need of some attention, length approx. 25cm. Sold for £22, Hansons Auctioneers, September.

A boxed tinplate battery operated toy fire command car made by Nomura (T.N.) of Japan. In original but played with condition. Some parts detached but present. Missing aerial. Untested. Original box in poor condition. Sold for £20, Hansons Auctioneers, September.

YOUR MONTHLY MODEL COLLECTING MAGAZINE

UK's No.1 magazine for model collectors

Introduction to...
TV & Film

O ver the past couple of decades, TV and film collectables have become an increasingly dominant part of the collecting market. Head to many of the toy fairs throughout the UK and you'll see an increasing amount of *Star Wars* figures, Transformers and Teenage Mutant Ninja Turtles dotted among the more traditional diecast cars, model railways and toy soldiers. Even more exciting is the fact that some TV and film collectables are now making big money at auction, with rare *Star Wars* figures regularly realising thousands.

Along with *Star Wars*, some of the more desireable TV and film pieces include James Bond memorabilia, toys based on the works of Gerry Anderson (such as *Thunderbirds* and *Captain Scarlet*), *Doctor Who* and superheroes, like Batman and Superman. Ignoring *Star Wars*, the reason why many of these collectables are so sought after is because they've been entertaining children since the 1960s and toy manufacturers have been making products inspired by these films or TV series for decades.

As a result, many of the most sought after pieces are those that were produced in the '60s, such as the iconic Aston Martin DB5 from Goldfinger, as made by Corgi.

However, in recent years there has been growing interest in TV and film collectables from the late 1970s and '80s. As that generation reaches their 30s and 40s, they're keen to pick up the toys they remember from their youth, meaning there's an emerging market of more 'modern' items based on the likes of *Transformers*, *Thundercats*, *He-Man* and even *Mighty Morphin' Power Rangers*. Prices for these toys are creeping up all the time and they're certainly likely to increase as more collectors realise their potential value.

Of course, *Star Wars* is still the major player in the TV and film market, with some very rare action figures selling for more than £10,000. The most valuable pieces tend to be those produced by UK company Palitoy for the original film in 1977. Unlike the follow-ups, no one predicted how popular the merchandise would be and, as a result, only a limited number of toys were produced. By the time *Return of the Jedi* was released in 1983, American maker Kenner was flooding the market to capitalise on the trilogy's success, meaning these toys are less valuable, in comparison.

However, perhaps more so than any other collectable, condition is absolutely everything with TV and film memorabilia. Serious collectors will look for action figures on their original card, with the plastic bubble still intact, no tears or scuffs to the card and even like it if the hole to hang the toy from the toyshop shelf remains unpunched. Having a toy in this kind of mint condition can quickly add hundreds to its value.

There are even those that get their toys 'graded' by a company like UK Graders. These companies closely inspect the toy in question and then rate it out of 10, depending upon the condition of the box and the model inside. Once graded it's then sealed inside a protective case and the rating is clearly displayed on the outside. In America this is becoming an increasingly popular way of demonstrating that a collectable is the 'real deal'. ∎

Planet of the Apes TV show Galen figure, carded. Sold for £110, Stacey's Auctioneers, October.

Star Wars carded r5-d4 figure by Kenner, carded. Sold for £160, Stacey's Auctioneers, October.

An A-Team The Bad Guy figure, carded. Sold for £60, Stacey's Auctioneers, October.

Corgi Juniors No 3021 Crimefighters Set, comprising Batmobile, Kojak's Buick, 007 Lotus, Starsky & Hutch Ford Torino, Batcopter and Spiderman's Copter. Excellent in excellent box. Sold for £150, Warwick & Warwick, November.

Star Wars Anakin Skywalker tri Logo figure, carded. Sold for £60, Stacey's Auctioneers, October.

Star Wars carded Klaatu figure, carded. Sold for £60, Stacey's Auctioneers, October.

The A-Team Murdock figure, carded. Sold for £60, Stacey's Auctioneers, October.

Dinky Toys No 100 Thunderbirds Lady Penelope's FAB 1, pink, missile, sliding clear roof, cast hubs, gold interior with Lady Penelope and Parker figures. Good plus in good plus box with inner plinth. Sold for £130, Warwick & Warwick, November.

Star Wars Lobot carded Kenner figure, carded. Sold for £60, Stacey's Auctioneers, October.

Star Wars general Madine figure, carded. Sold for £45, Stacey's Auctioneers, October.

A-Team figure B.A.Baracus figure, carded. Sold for £130, Stacey's Auctioneers, October.

Corgi Toys No 261 James Bond 007 Aston Martin DB5, with James Bond and 2 bandit figures and 'Top Secret' instructions. Excellent in excellent box and inner plinth. Sold for £120, Warwick & Warwick, November.

Star Wars carded Prune Face, tri logo figure, carded. Sold for £50, Stacey's Auctioneers, October.

Star Wars Rebel Commander Figure by Kenner. Blister is coming away from the card. Sold for £50, Stacey's Auctioneers, October.

The A-Team Faceman figure, carded. Sold for £90, Stacey's Auctioneers, October.

Corgi Toys No 292 Starsky & Hutch Ford Torino, red body with white stripe, pale yellow interior, 4-spoke wheels, complete with original figures. Excellent plus in good plus window box. Sold for £100, Vectis, December.

Star Wars Princess Leia in combat poncho, Kenner figure, carded. Sold for £70, Stacey's Auctioneers, October.

Star Wars Stormtrooper (hoth Gear) carded, hole in back of card. Sold for £80, Stacey's Auctioneers, October.

Star Trek Mr Spock figure from 1974, carded. Sold for £120, Stacey's Auctioneers, October.

Corgi Toys No 290 Kojak Buick Regal, metallic bronze body, ivory interior, scarce 4-spoke wheels, complete with dark grey Crocker figure & bald head Kojak figure. Excellent to excellent plus in good plus window box complete. Sold for £120, Vectis, December.

DIECAST   RAILWAYS   TOY FIGURES   TINPLATE   TV & FILM   OTHERS   EBUYS

Corgi Toys No 267 Batmobile, gloss black body with bare metal front slasher blade & operating button, bare metal rear jet exhaust, light blue windows, dayglo orange interior complete with both original figures, brass cast hubs. Good plus in fair box. Sold for £150, Vectis, December.

Corgi Toys No 261 James Bond's Aston Martin DB5 original empty box only, good plus with a couple of small tears to end flaps, complete with excellent plus inner pictorial card display stand, secret Instruction leaflet & single bandit figure. Sold for £80, Vectis, December.

A vintage 1983 carded Palitoy Star Wars 3 3/4 action figure of 'Klaatu'. The figure is unpunched on a 65A back card and is UKG graded - card 80%; bubble 80%; figure 90%; overall 80%. Sold for £80, British Toy Auctions, January.

A boxed vintage Star Wars ROTJ Jabba The Hut Playset by Kenner. The item appears to be in excellent condition and is unchecked for completeness. The playset is within a good overall box with some taping, scuffs plus age related wear and tear. The set also contains its instruction sheet. Sold for £85, British Toy Auctions, January.

A boxed vintage Palitoy Star Wars Empire Strikes Back 'At-At'. The model appears to be in good overall condition with signs of play and use and has both of its chin guns. Box is in fair plus condition with some creasing, tears and general storage wear. Sold for £95, British Toy Auctions, January.

A boxed vintage Star Wars TESB Millennium Falcon. The model, marked CPG Kenner to the underside has play wear but overall appears generally to be in good condition and is unchecked for completeness. The box is in fair plus - good condition with some taping, scuffs and storage imperfections. Sold for £80, British Toy Auctions, January.

A boxed vintage Star Wars ROTJ tri-logo B-Wing Fighter Vehicle. In very good overall condition with signs of play and use, and is marked LFL 1980 to the underside. The set contains two posters, and is presented within a good plus box with some taping, scuffs and general wear. Sold for £220, British Toy Auctions, January.

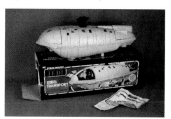

A boxed vintage Star Wars ROTJ Rebel Transport vehicle. The vehicle has play wear and is unchecked for completeness but appears to be in good condition, with original creased and torn instruction leaflet. The box is fair plus with general age related wear and tear. Sold for £50, British Toy Auctions, January.

A boxed vintage Star Wars ROTJ Scout Walker. Item appears to be in good overall condition with signs of play and use. The original box is good overall condition with some taping and storage imperfections. A very displayable piece! Sold for £70, British Toy Auctions, January.

A boxed vintage Palitoy Star Wars Empire Strikes Back Slave I - Bobba Fett's Spaceship. In good condition with original instruction sheet, a sheet of decals together with 'Frozen Han Solo'. Box is in fair plus to ood overall condition with some creasing, tears and general storage wear. Sold for £100, British Toy Auctions, January.

A boxed vintage 12" Poseable Luke Skywalker figure #33326. The figure in an opened box, in good overall condition despite signs of play and comes with utility belt only. The box is in fair plus - good condition missing its insert and has storage wear. Sold for £85, British Toy Auctions, January.

A boxed vintage Star Wars 12" R2-D2 figure. Appears to be in good condition with signs of play, is marked 'GMFGI 1978 Kenner'. The figure is missing accessories. The box in fair good condition with some general storage. Sold for £170, British Toy Auctions, January.

A boxed vintage Denys Fisher Star Wars 12" C3PO figure. Appears to be in good condition and is marked 'General Mills Fun Group 1978 Made in Hong Kong'. Box is in fair plus condition with some creasing. Sold for £200, British Toy Auctions, January.

A boxed vintage Denys Fisher Star Wars 12" poseable Stormtrooper figure. Appears in good overall with signs of play and use, and is marked 'General Mills Fun Group Inc 1978 Made in Hong Kong'. Box is fair plus with some taping. Sold for £160, British Toy Auctions, January.

A boxed vintage Denys Fisher Star Wars 12" poseable Chewbacca figure. The figure appears to be in good overall condition with signs of play and use, and is marked 'GMFGI 1978 Made in Hong Kong'. The figure has its Cross Bow Laser Rifle but is missing its belt and ammunition cartridges. The box appears to be in fair condition with some tears, creasing, taping, and general storage wear. Sold for £110, British Toy Auctions, January.

Galoob vintage 1983 A-Team Templeton Peck Face 6" figure, mint, within near mint (yellowed, lifting to one corner) bubble, upon excellent un-punched card. Sold for £90, Vectis, January.

A boxed vintage Denys Fisher Star Wars 15" poseable Darth Vader figure with Light Sabre and Cape. The figure appears to be in good overall condition with signs of play and use, and is marked 'GMFGI 1978 Made in Hong Kong'. The box appears to be in fair plus to good condition with some taping, scuffing and general storage wear. Sold for £160, British Toy Auctions, January.

Two boxed vintage Palitoy Kenner Star Wars vehicles. Lot contains a Star wars ROTJ Y-Wing Fighter which appears in good overall condition with signs of play wear marked Kenner to the underside, presented in a good box with some taping and age related wear; together with a Star Wars X-Wing Fighter. The vehicle has varying degrees of play wear and appears incomplete marked Kenner to the underside. The box is in poor condition with creasing, missing flaps and storage imperfections. Sold for £130, British Toy Auctions, January.

Corgi Toys No 336 James Bond Toyota 2000GT from the film 'You Only Live Twice', white body, two figures, rocket launchers in boot. Mint in mint box, with secret instructions envelope, Corgi club/ instruction leaflet, cloth badge, and inner packing ring. Sold for £560, C&T Auctions. January.

Corgi Toys The Avengers Gift Set 40, Steed's Bentley, green body, red wire wheels and Emma Peel's white Lotus Elan S2, with original figures and three umbrellas. Near mint in excellent box with very good inner tray and Corgi Club leaflet. Sold for £820, C&T Auctions. January.

Corgi Toys No 497 The Man From UNCLE 'Thrush Buster' Oldsmobile, metallic blue, cast wheels, plastic chrome spot lights and 'Waverly' ring. Mint on excellent inner card display stand in excellent box, with inner white packing card, packing ring and card ring to roof, and Corgi leaflet. Sold for £420, C&T Auctions. January.

Corgi Toys Batmobile and Batboat on Trailer, black early No 267 Batmobile with red motifs to wheels, includes Batman and Robin figures, black No 107 Batboat on gold trailer, plus opened packet containing 10 x rockets, 6 of which are still on their sprue. Good plus to excellent in fair to good packaging. Sold for £520, Vectis, February.

Corgi Toys No 270 "James Bond" Aston Martin DB5, silver, red interior with James Bond figure only, and tyre slashers. Good plus in fair to good 1st issue wing flap presentation bubble pack (missing inner card and instruction pack). Sold for £120, Vectis, March.

Corgi No 96655 "James Bond" Aston Martin DB5, silver, red interior and tyre slashers, 1995 reissue model. Mint in excellent plus striped window box. Sold for £45, Vectis, March.

Corgi Toys "Chitty Chitty Bang Bang", recent limited edition production replica, includes 4 figures with opening stabilisers and spare rear stabiliser for separate attachment. Near mint, including leaflet, certificate and instruction slip, in excellent card box. Sold for £60, Vectis, March.

Corgi Toys No 805 1912 Rolls Royce Silver Ghost "Hardy Boys", multi coloured vehicle with 5x figures. Near mint in good plus window box. Sold for £180, Vectis, March.

Dinky Toys No 100 Lady Penelope's FAB1, pink, with clear sliding roof, Lady Penelope & Parker figures, early issue with silver headlamp surrounds and pink bands to the canopy, with original rocket and harpoons with detail plastic hubs. Good plus to excellent in fair card box with inner card display stand. Sold for £170, Vectis, March.

Playmates 1988 vintage Teenage Mutant Ninja Turtles Donatello figure, CAS Graded 85 - card 85, bubble 80, figure 85, upon un-punched 10 back card. Sold for £160, Vectis, March.

Playmates 1988 vintage Teenage Mutant Ninja Turtles Michelangelo figure CAS Graded 85 - card 85, bubble 85, figure 80, upon un-punched 10 back card, with statement of archival. Sold for £150, Vectis, March.

Playmates 1988 vintage Teenage Mutant Ninja Turtles Raphael figure, CAS Graded 80 - card 80, bubble 80, figure 85, upon un-punched 10 back card. Sold for £150, Vectis, March.

Playmates 1988 vintage Teenage Mutant Ninja Turtles Shredder figure, AFA Graded 75 EX+/NM card 75, bubble 85, figure 85, upon un-punched 10 back card. Sold for £140, Vectis, March.

Playmates 1988 vintage Teenage Mutant Ninja Turtles Splinter figure, AFA Graded 75 EX+/NM card 85, bubble 75, figure 80, upon un-punched 10 back card. Sold for £130, Vectis, March.

Playmates 1988 vintage Teenage Mutant Ninja Turtles April O'Neil figure, mint, within near mint bubble, upon excellent (sticker residue) un-punched 10 back card. Includes acrylic slide bottom case. Sold for £80, Vectis, March.

| DIECAST | RAILWAYS | TOY FIGURES | TINPLATE | TV & FILM | OTHERS | EBUYS |

Playmates 1988 vintage Teenage Mutant Ninja Turtles Bebop figure, mint, within near mint bubble, upon excellent (crease to reverse) un-punched 10 back card. Includes acrylic slide bottom case. Sold for £170, Vectis, March.

Playmates 1988 vintage Teenage Mutant Ninja Turtles Rocksteady figure, mint, within near mint bubble, upon excellent (crease to reverse and minor surface wear) un-punched 10 back card. Includes acrylic slide bottom case. Sold for £170, Vectis, March.

Playmates 1988 vintage Teenage Mutant Ninja Turtles Foot Soldier figure, mint, within near mint bubble, upon excellent (crease to reverse) un-punched 10 back card. Includes acrylic slide bottom case. Sold for £150, Vectis, March.

Playmates 1989 vintage Teenage Mutant Ninja Turtles Krang figure, mint, within near mint bubble, upon excellent (crease to reverse) un-punched 14 back card. Includes acrylic slide bottom case. Sold for £100, Vectis, March.

Playmates 1989 vintage Teenage Mutant Ninja Turtles Baxter Stockman figure, mint, within near mint bubble, upon excellent (crease to front) un-punched 14 back card. Includes acrylic slide bottom case. Sold for £110, Vectis, March.

Playmates 1989 vintage Teenage Mutant Ninja Turtles Ace Duck figure, mint, within near mint bubble, upon near mint un-punched 14 back card. Includes acrylic slide bottom case. Sold for £80, Vectis, March.

Playmates 1989 vintage Teenage Mutant Ninja Turtles Genghis Frog figure, mint, within near mint bubble, upon excellent (crease to front and reverse) un-punched 14 back card. Includes acrylic slide bottom case. Sold for £70, Vectis, March.

Playmates 1989 vintage Wacky Action Teenage Mutant Ninja Turtles Wacky Walkin Mouse figure, mint, within near mint bubble, upon excellent (crease to front) un-punched 21 back card. Sold for £90, Vectis, March.

Playmates 1989 vintage Wacky Action Teenage Mutant Ninja Turtles Sewer Swimmin Donatello figure, mint, within near mint bubble, upon excellent (crease to front) un-punched 21 back card. Sold for £90, Vectis, March.

Playmates 1989 vintage Wacky Action Teenage Mutant Ninja Turtles Breakfightin Raphael figure, mint, within near mint bubble, upon excellent (crease to front) un-punched 21 back card. Sold for £90, Vectis, March.

Playmates 1989 vintage Wacky Action Teenage Mutant Ninja Turtles Rock N Roll Michelangelo figure, mint, within near mint bubble, upon excellent (crease to front) un-punched 21 back card. Sold for £70, Vectis, March.

Playmates 1990 vintage Wacky Action Teenage Mutant Ninja Turtles Sword Slicin Leoardo figure, mint, within excellent bubble, upon excellent un-punched 37 back card. Sold for £90, Vectis, March.

Playmates 1990 vintage Wacky Action Teenage Mutant Ninja Turtles Slice N Dice Shredder figure, mint, within excellent (slight dent) bubble, upon good (creases to front) un-punched 44 back card. Sold for £45, Vectis, March.

Kenner Star Wars vintage C-3PO 3 3/4" figure, AFA Graded 80 NM+ card 80, bubble 85, figure 85, upon un-punched 12 C back card. Sold for £620, Vectis, March.

Kenner Star Wars vintage Han Solo LARGE HEAD 3 3/4" figure, AFA Graded 80 NM - card 80, bubble 80, figure 85, upon un-punched 12 C back card. Sold for £1200, Vectis, March.

Kenner Star Wars vintage Princess Leia Organa 3 3/4" figure, AFA Graded 80 - card 85, bubble 80, figure 80, upon un-punched 12 B back card. Sold for £1200, Vectis, March.

Kenner Star Wars vintage Stormtrooper 3 3/4" figure, AFA Graded 80 - card 80, bubble 80, figure 80, upon un-punched 12 C back card. Sold for £950, Vectis, March.

Kenner Star Wars vintage Darth Vader 3 3/4" figure, AFA Graded 80 - card 80, bubble 85, figure 85, upon un-punched 12 C back card. Sold for £1600, Vectis, March.

Kenner Star Wars vintage R2-D2 3 3/4" figure, AFA Graded 80 - card 80, bubble 80, figure 80, upon un-punched 12 C back card. Sold for £1100, Vectis, March.

Kenner Star Wars vintage Ben Obi-Wan Kenobi (white Hair) 3 3/4" figure, AFA Graded 85 - card 85, bubble 85, figure 85, upon un-punched 12 C back card. Sold for £1500, Vectis, March.

Kenner Star Wars vintage Luke Skywalker 3 3/4" figure, CAS Graded 80 - card 85, bubble 80, figure 80, upon un-punched 12 A back card (comes with CAS certificate of archival). Sold for £1700, Vectis, March.

Kenner Star Wars vintage Jawa 3 3/4" figure, CAS Graded 80+ card 85, bubble 70, figure 85, upon un-punched 12 C back card. Sold for £680, Vectis, March.

Kenner Star Wars vintage Chewbacca 3 3/4" figure, CAS Graded 80 - card 85, bubble 75, figure 85, upon un-punched 12 C back card. Sold for £640, Vectis, March.

Kenner Star Wars vintage Death Squad Commander 3 3/4" figure, mint, within good bubble, upon good plus (one crease) un-punched 12 B back card. Includes slide bottom acrylic case. Sold for £660, Vectis, March.

Kenner Star Wars vintage Sand People 3 3/4" figure, mint, within near mint bubble, upon excellent to near mint un-punched 12 B back card. Includes slide bottom acrylic case. Sold for £1200, Vectis, March.

Kenner Star Wars vintage R5-D4 3 3/4" figure, near mint, within good bubble, upon excellent to near mint (some surface creasing to reverse) un-punched 20 G back card. Includes slide bottom acrylic case. Sold for £520, Vectis, March.

Kenner Star Wars vintage Greedo 3 3/4" figure, mint, within excellent bubble, upon excellent (some surface creasing to reverse) un-punched 20 C back card. Includes slide bottom acrylic case. Sold for £620, Vectis, March.

Kenner Star Wars vintage Snaggletooth 3 3/4" figure, AFA 85 NM+ card 80, bubble 85, figure 85, upon un-punched 21 B back card. Sold for £1300, Vectis, March.

Corgi Toys 258 The "Saints" Volvo P.1800, in very good to excellent original condition, some slight paint chipping, complete with Corgi Collectors Club leaflet, yellow and blue illustrated box complete with all end flaps, in excellent original condition. Sold for £300, C&T Auctioneers, May.

Corgi Toys 261 James Bond Aston Martin D.B.5 from the Film "Goldfinger" gold body, with ejector seat, bandit and James Bond figures, rear bullet screen, retractable machine guns, in very good to excellent original unboxed condition, a couple of tiny paint chips to roof. Sold for £85, C&T Auctioneers, May.

Corgi Toys 266 "Chitty Chitty Bang Bang", complete with "Caractacus Potts, Truly Scrumptious, Jeremy and Jemima" figures, gold/ chrome/bronze body, model is in mint original condition, with back and front wings, including inner plastic cloud, card cloud display, original box. Sold for £120, C&T Auctioneers, May.

Boxed Corgi Toys 1st issue 267 Rocket Firing Batmobile, with "Batman & Robin" figures, in excellent original condition, including an excellent original inner card stand. Complete with opened instruction pack containing folded leaflet, used cloth lapel badge, action features leaflet and 10 yellow original missiles (5 loose-5 still on sprue) Corgi model club leaflet, original outer blue and yellow carded picture box is in good condition, complete with all end flaps, some age/edge wear. Sold for £460, C&T Auctioneers, May.

Corgi Toys 277 The Monkees Monkeemobile, red body, white roof, cast wheels, with figures of Mike, Mikey, Davey & Pete, model is in near mint original condition, with an excellent original window box, vintage price label to front of box. Sold for £160, C&T Auctioneers, May.

Pre-Production Palitoy vintage Action Force British Commando 3 3/4" Prototype Metal figure, used for display at the British Toy Fair 1982. The individual components have been cast in metal from rubber moulds, constructed then finally hand-painted, good plus (some minor paint chips). Comes with a certificate from Palitoy manager and lead designer Bob Brechin. Sold for £600, Vectis, September.

Pre-Production Palitoy vintage Action Force Deep Sea Diver 3 3/4" Prototype Metal figure, used for display at the British Toy Fair 1982. The individual components have been cast in metal from rubber moulds, constructed then finally hand-painted, good (some paint chips). Comes with a certificate from Palitoy manager and lead designer Bob Brechin. Sold for £400, Vectis, September.

Pre-Production Palitoy vintage Action Force German Stormtrooper 3 3/4" Prototype Metal figure, used for display at the British Toy Fair 1982. The individual components have been cast in metal from rubber moulds, constructed then finally hand-painted, good plus (some minor paint chips). Comes with a certificate from Palitoy manager and lead designer Bob Brechin. Sold for £580, Vectis, September.

Kenner Star Wars Return of the Jedi vintage Boba Fett 3 3/4" figure, UKG Graded Y80% subs card 85, bubble 80 figure 90, upon un-punched 77 back card. Sold for £2200, Vectis, September.

Palitoy Star Wars Return of the Jedi Tri-Logo vintage Han Solo 3 3/4" figure, UKG Graded 85% subs card 85, bubble 85, figure 85, upon punched 77 back card. Sold for £580, Vectis, September.

Palitoy Star Wars The Empire Strikes Back vintage Luke Skywalker Bespin (brown hair) 3 3/4" figure, UKG Graded 85% subs card 85, bubble 85, figure 85, upon punched 41 back card. Sold for £1300, Vectis, September.

Palitoy Star Wars vintage C-3PO 3 3/4" figure, mint, within near mint bubble, upon near mint (minor crease to reverse) un-punched 12 back card. Sold for £900, Vectis, September.

Kenner Star Wars vintage Jawa Vinyl Cape 3 3/4" figure, fair complete, cape has split under one arm that has been repaired. Sold for £520, Vectis, September.

Kenner Star Wars vintage Yak Face 3 3/4" figure, fair (paint wear to hands and boots). Sold for £220, Vectis, September.

Kenner Star Wars vintage Luke Skywalker Stormtrooper outfit 3 3/4" figure, good complete (blue black blaster). Sold for £220, Vectis, September.

Palitoy Star Wars vintage The Death Star Play-set, good plus complete, within fair opened box. Sold for £950, Vectis, September.

Kenner Star Wars Return of the Jedi vintage Ben Obi-Wan Kenobi 3 3/4" figure upon Jawa 65 back card, this is a mock-up/ miscard, 100% factory sealed. Figure is mint, card is in good condition (some creasing and edge wear) punched, bubble is good (minor denting to one corner), only know example of this combination. Sold for £6400, Vectis, September.

Harbert (Italian) Star Wars vintage Han Solo Jan Solo 3 3/4" figure, mint, within fair (crack to top) bubble, upon excellent un-punched 12 back card. Sold for £2100, Vectis, September.

Toltoys (Australia) Star Wars vintage R2-D2 3 3/4" figure, mint, within good plus (dented) bubble, upon good (small tare to bottom, creasing and edge wear) un-punched 12 back card. Sold for £5400, Vectis, September.

Toltoys (Australia) Star Wars vintage C-3PO 3 3/4" figure, mint, within excellent bubble, upon fair (sticker tare, creasing and edge wear) punched 12 back card. Sold for £4800, Vectis, September.

Toltoys (Australia) Star Wars vintage Princess Leia 3 3/4" figure, mint, within good (dented) bubble, upon fair (creasing and edge wear) punched 12 back card. Sold for £5800, Vectis, September.

Toltoys (Australia) Star Wars vintage Darth Vader 3 3/4" figure, mint, within good (yellowed and dented) bubble, upon fair (creasing and edge wear) punched 20 back card. Sold for £10,000, Vectis, September.

Kenner (Canadian) La Guerre Des Etoiles Star Wars vintage C-3PO 3 3/4" figure, mint, within excellent bubble, upon good plus (minor creasing and edge wear) punched 12 back card. Sold for £3400, Vectis, September.

Kenner (Canadian) La Guerre Des Etoiles Star Wars vintage R2-D2 3 3/4" figure, mint, within good (dented) bubble, upon good (creasing, staple holes and edge wear) punched 12 back card. Sold for £2200, Vectis, September.

Takara (Japan) Star Wars vintage Princess Leia 3 3/4" figure, mint, within excellent bubble, upon good (punch hole, pin holes and edge wear) punched 12 back card. Sold for £2400, Vectis, September.

PBP (Spain) Star Wars The Empire Strikes Back El Imperio Contraataca vintage Lando Calrissian 3 3/4" figure, mint, within excellent bubble, upon fair (ink touch up around punch hole and edge wear) punched 45 back card. Sold for £2900, Vectis, September.

Clipper Star Wars The Empire Strikes Back vintage Hammerhead 3 3/4" figure, mint, within near mint bubble, upon excellent punched 45 back card. Sold for £850, Vectis, September.

Kenner Star Wars The Power Of The Force vintage Han Solo Carbonite 3 3/4" figure, mint, within excellent (yellowed) bubble, upon good plus to excellent (edge wear) un-punched 92 back card. Sold for £540, Vectis, September.

LIMITED EDITION MAGAZINES
PERFECT FOR COLLECTING

The Aircraft of the USAF in Europe

This 132-page special collectors magazine records and shows a picture of EVERY military aircraft used by the United States forces while they have been stationed in Europe. All 625 of them. Subject matter includes fighter and bomber aircraft from the Great War, World War Two, the Cold War and more recent conflicts in the Gulf and Afghanistan as well as training aircraft, cargo flights and even the racing aircraft that competed for the interwar Pulitzer Trophy. It is intended to appeal to both enthusiasts and those with a passing interest in aeroplanes.

NEW! **£9.99**

Battle of Britain in Colour

A unique and stunning 164-page high-quality collectors magazine showcasing the work of colourisation artist Richard Molloy and telling the story of the Battle of Britain through colourised images from the period.

£8.99

Aircraft of the RAF

Using a mix of archive images and contemporary photographs this 132-page special collector's magazine tells the story of the RAF from the flimsy canvas and wire biplanes the fledgling air arm inherited when it was formed through to the modern cutting-edge aircraft of today.

£7.99

Tanks of WWII

Tanks of WWII is a lavishly illustrated 164-page guide to 178 Allied and Axis tank models, variants and prototypes. With blueprints and technical details, plus famous tank commanders, the significant tank battles of WWII and the best tank museums to visit.

NEW! **£9.99**

To buy your special edition simply go to these websites:

Printed issues go to: **militaria.ma/bookazines**

Digital issues go to:
pocketmags.com/the-armourer-magazine/specialissues

Introduction to...
everything else!

Well, where do you begin with such a broad category? This section covers a massive selection of toys that simply don't fit in any of our previous categories. Over the next few pages, you can see prices for boardgames, Meccano, LEGO, Subbuteo, plastic robots, slot cars... the list goes on.

However, just because they're all grouped together doesn't mean they're any less valuable than those collectables we've seen on the previous pages and, as you'll see, many of these pieces can certainly hold their own at auction! It would be impossible for us to give advice for every single type of collectable in this section, so instead we'll highlight a few choice examples.

Boardgames seem an obvious place to start because there are so many, with some dating all the way back to Victorian times. In fact, expert Alan Goldsmith, owner of the House on the Hill Toy Museum, Stansted, has tipped boardgames to become one of the more sought after items in years to come. He gives a couple of reasons for this train

of thought - firstly many of the older examples from the early 20th century were produced in remarkably small numbers. Often printers would take a break from publishing books or other materials and spend a week making new boardgames. As such, the numbers were remarkably small, making some boardgames particularly collectable. His second reason is that boardgames appeal to both male and female collectors, which helps to expand the market when they're sold at auction. If you're interested in

finding out more about vintage boardgames, consider picking up Alan's book, *Vintage and Collectable Board and Table Top Games*. Moving away from boardgames, Meccano is another big hitter at auction. First conceived by Frank Hornby in 1898, Meccano went on to be one of the most popular toys of all time. Hornby's idea was simple - instead of giving a child one toy, why not give them the means to create a whole range of models with just a few pieces. In fact, without the success of Meccano we wouldn't have seen Dinky

Toys or Hornby model railways, which were both spin offs from the company originally founded by Frank Hornby in 1908. In terms of value, the early pre-War Meccano sets in their distinctive wooden chests are the ones sought after by serious collectors. However, there's also a very strong market for promotional models, such as ferris wheels and windmills, that were built at the Meccano factory before being shipped off to toyshops across the UK.

Finally, it's worth mentioning Action Man and the numerous figures and accessories produced by Palitoy. Although Action Man's popularity may be on the decline, according to some, there's still a dedicated community of Action Man collectors willing to pay top whack for rare pieces. Interestingly, it's not just the figures that are worth picking up, as some of the outfits sold separately are also considered highly collectable. Often the outfits will be grouped into large lots, so it's worth closely inspecting the auctioneer's description to see whether there's a hidden gem among the other Action Man uniforms.

Vintage Pelham Puppets marionette boy, in a damaged box. Sold for £15, Pro Auctions, November.

Vintage Pelham Puppets marionette Bengo Boxer Dog, in a box. Sold for £20, Pro Auctions, November.

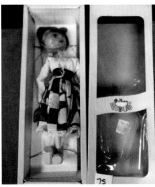

Vintage Pelham Puppets marionette Mitzi, in a box. Sold for £15, Pro Auctions, November.

Meccano Showman's traction engine, electrically illuminated, finely detailed, excellent. Sold for £170, Lacy, Scott & Knight, November.

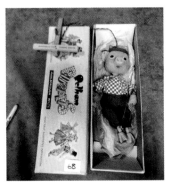

Vintage Pelham Puppets Marionette type Ss Pinky, in a box. Sold for £35, Pro Auctions, November.

Vintage Pelham Puppets marionette Golly, in a box. Sold for £45, Pro Auctions, November.

Vintage Pelham Puppets marionette Wicked Witch, in a damaged box. Sold for £20, Pro Auctions, November.

Meccano No. 7 outfit, circa 1929/30, green box, appears substantially complete, repro handles on front drawers. Sold for £550, Lacy, Scott & Knight, November.

Pelham Puppet Dutch Girl Ss string marionette, from 1960. Sold for £15, Pro Auctions, November.

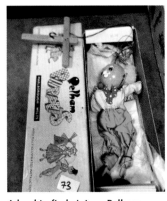

A hard to find vintage Pelham Puppets marionette Old Man, in a box. Sold for £30, Pro Auctions, November.

Meccano window display model Ferris wheel, 1950s, electric powered, good to very good. Sold for £100, Lacy, Scott & Knight, November.

Meccano No. 7 outfit oak cabinet, circa 1925, full of parts, mainly nickel, showing some signs of rust. Sold for £1050, Lacy, Scott & Knight, November.

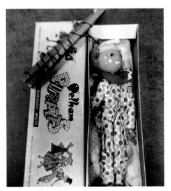

Vintage Pelham Puppets marionette SS6 clown, in a box. Sold for £20, Pro Auctions, November.

Vintage Pelham Puppets marionette Gretel, in a box. Sold for £20, Pro Auctions, November.

Meccano window display model dockside crane, electrically powered, circa early 1950s, excellent. Sold for £120, Lacy, Scott & Knight, November.

Meccano No. 10 outfit, green cabinet, circa 1938, blue/gold, appears substantially complete and used. Sold for £550, Lacy, Scott & Knight, November.

DIECAST | RAILWAYS | TOY FIGURES | TINPLATE | TV & FILM | OTHERS | EBUYS

Meccano No. 6 outfit, green cabinet, circa 1930/31, complete, majority of parts appear unused, repro where card, correct dome headed bolts. Sold for £520, Lacy, Scott & Knight, November.

Meccano 'K' outfit, green cabinet, circa 1936, containing a substantial collection of blue/gold parts. Sold for £280, Lacy, Scott & Knight, November.

Meccano No. 3 storage cabinet, red, complete with tray containing quantity of blue/gold Meccano in average/used condition. Sold for £110, Lacy, Scott & Knight, November.

Meccano No. 9A accessory outfit, box in poor condition, containing miscellaneous 1950 red/green parts all poor to fair. Sold for £160, Lacy, Scott & Knight, November.

Meccano No. 8 outfit, circa 1960 appears complete generally good used condition. Sold for £75, Lacy, Scott & Knight, November.

Meccano No. 1 Elektron, 1933 outfit substantially complete, good condition, without manual. Sold for £50, Lacy, Scott & Knight, November.

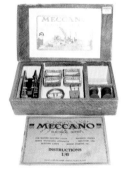

Meccano Electrical outfit, 1920 with manual, complete but without accumulator. Sold for £270, Lacy, Scott & Knight, November.

Meccano France Kemex No. 3 outfit, with instructions, appears complete and unused, excellent. Box in good condition but one side of lid missing. Sold for £150, Lacy, Scott & Knight, November.

Large box with 3 layers Meccano gold/blue, original base, repro trays and lid, generally good used condition. Sold for £250, Lacy, Scott & Knight, November.

Uncanny X-Men #101, 1976, Marvel, UK price variant. The origin and first appearance of Phoenix (Jean Grey), Black Tom Cassidy and Juggernaut appearances. Dave Cockrum cover and art. Flat/unfolded. Sold for £220, Excalibur Auctions, December.

Uncanny X-Men #100, 1976, Marvel, UK price variant. The original X-Men verses the new X-Men. Partial origin of Phoenix, Dave Cockrum cover and art. Flat/unfolded. Sold for £38, Excalibur Auctions, December.

Uncanny X-Men #99, 1976, Marvel, UK price variant. First appearance Black Tom Cassidy, Sentinels appearance. Dave Cockrum cover and art. Flat/unfolded. Sold for £65, Excalibur Auctions, December.

Uncanny X-Men #97, 1976, MARVEL, UK price variant. First appearance of Lilandra, Havok and Polaris, Eric the Red. Dave Cockrum art, flat/unfolded. Sold for £32, Excalibur Auctions, December.

Uncanny X-Men #135, 1980, Marvel, UK price variant. Second appearance Dark Phoenix, first appearance of Senator Robert Kelly and Reed Richards, Thing, Spider-Man, Doctor Strange, and Silver Surfer cameo appearances. John Byrne cover and interior art, flat/unfolded. Sold for £15, Excalibur Auctions, December.

Uncanny X-Men #136, 1980, Marvel, UK price variant. Lilandra appearance, President Jimmy Carter appears in one panel. John Byrne cover and interior art, flat/unfolded. Sold for £15, Excalibur Auctions, December.

Uncany X-Men #133, 1980, Marvel, UK price variant. The very first solo Wolverine cover, Hellfire Club (Sebastian Shaw, Harry Leland, Donald Pierce, and Mastermind) appearance. John Byrne and Terry Austin cover and interior art. Flat/unfolded. Sold for £25, Excalibur Auctions, December.

Uncanny X-Men #109, 1978, Marvel, UK price variant. First appearance of Vindicator, aka Guardian, called Weapon Alpha here. Dave Cockrum cover with John Byrne interior art, flat/unfolded. Sold for £25, Excalibur Auctions, December.

Daredevil #7, 1965, Marvel, UK cover price. First appearance of Daredevil's signature red costume and Sub-Mariner appearance. Wally Wood cover and interior art, flat/unfolded. Sold for £90, Excalibur Auctions, December.

Daredevil #12, 1966, Marvel, UK price variant. First appearance of the Plunderer, Ka-Zar and Zabu. Cover and interior art by John Romita Sr, over layouts by Jack Kirby. Flat/unfolded. Sold for £15, Excalibur Auctions, December.

Daredevil #13, 1966, Marvel, UK price variant. Origin of Ka-Zar and the Plunderer, Zabu appearance. Cover and interior art by John Romita Sr, over layouts by Jack Kirby. Flat/unfolded. Sold for £28, Excalibur Auctions, December.

Daredevil #16, 1966, Marvel, UK price variant. Spider-Man crossover, first appearance of the Masked Marauder. Cover and interior art by John Romita Sr, his first work on Spider-Man. Flat/unfolded. Sold for £35, Excalibur Auctions, December.

Detective Comics: Batman #359, 1967, DC, UK cover price. First appearance and origin of fan-favourite Batgirl (Barbara Gordon). First Silver Age appearance of the Killer Moth. Carmine Infantino and Murphy Anderson cover and interior art. Flat/unfolded. Sold for £380, Excalibur Auctions, December.

Justice League of America #21, 1963, DC, UK cover price. "Crisis on Earth-One" book re-introduces the Justice Society of America (Doctor Fate, Hourman, Atom, Hawkman, Green Lantern, Black Canary). Mike Sekowsky cover and interior art. Flat/unfolded. Sold for £50, Excalibur Auctions, December.

Justice League of America #29, 1964, DC, UK cover price. "Crisis on Earth-Three" story. First Silver Age appearance of Starman, first appearance of the Crime Syndicate. Mike Sekowsky cover and interior art, flat/unfolded. Sold for £42, Excalibur Auctions, December.

Lego Creator 10242 Expert Mini Cooper, an original sealed box set. Highly detailed. Sold for £150, East Bristol Auctions, January.

An original Lego Expert boxed set No 10220 'Volkswagen T1 Camper Van'. Highly detailed set with both instruction booklets included. Appears to be missing one front window, otherwise appears complete. Sold for £95, East Bristol Auctions, January.

An original Special Edition Lego Bionicle factory sealed boxed set No. 8940 'Karzahni'. Highly detailed set. Sold for £120, East Bristol Auctions, January.

An original Lego Star Wars factory sealed boxed set No. 7663 'Sith Infiltrator'. Highly detailed set with Darth Maul minifigure. Sold for £85, East Bristol Auctions, January.

An exclusive double-set Harry Potter factory sealed boxed sets No. 4757 Hogwarts Castle and 4729 Dumbledore's Office. Highly detailed sets factory sealed in cellophane. Sold for £400, East Bristol Auctions, January.

An original vintage 1987 boxed Monorail Lego set, with two way stations and a train a small cargo spacecraft, two containers and five Futuron astronaut minifigures. All in working order, complete with box and instructions. Rare. Sold for £300, East Bristol Auctions, January.

An original Lego Star Wars factory sealed boxed set No. 10026 'Naboo Starfighter'. Contents 100% complete and unused (still factory sealed in their original bags / boxes). Rare and sought after set. Sold for £550, East Bristol Auctions, January.

An original vintage Legoland No. 6276 Eldorado Pirate Fortress, with instruction booklet. The vendor assures us the set is 100% complete but unchecked. Sold for £95, East Bristol Auctions, January.

An original Lego Star Wars factory sealed boxed set No. 4479 'Tie Bomber'. A highly detailed set with Tie Fighter Pilot minifigure. Sold for £140, East Bristol Auctions, January.

A rare original Lego Star Wars boxed set, No. 10019 'Rebel Blockade Runner'. Contents 100% complete and unused (still factory sealed in their original bags / boxes). The outer box mint, only ever opened to check contents. Rare and sought after set. Sold for £800, East Bristol Auctions, January.

An original vintage Legoland pre-made set No. 6274 Caribbean Clipper Pirate Ship with instruction booklet. The vendor assures us the set is 100% complete although this remains unchecked. Sold for £120, East Bristol Auctions, January.

An original Lego Star Wars factory sealed boxed set No. 7657 AT-ST. Contents 100% complete and unused (still factory sealed in their original bags / boxes). A highly detailed set with AT-ST Driver minifigure. Sold for £70, East Bristol Auctions, January.

An original Lego Creator unboxed set No. 10248 Expert Ferrari F40, with instruction booklet present. Set appears complete but this remains unchecked. Sold for £55, East Bristol Auctions, January.

Lego DC Universe Superheroes 6860 The Batcave, original boxed set, with instructions and minifigures. Vendor assures us set is 100% complete and has recently been checked. Sold for £40, East Bristol Auctions, April.

A scarce Lego System factory sealed Star Wars set No. 7128 Speeder Bikes. Fully factory sealed, and unopened. Box in excellent condition. Sold for £45, East Bristol Auctions, April.

Lego Space 928 - Space Cruiser & Moon Base. An original vintage (1979) unboxed Lego Space set No. 928 Space Cruiser & Moon Base (Galaxy Explorer). Ccomplete but unchecked. Minifigures and instructions present. Sold for £85, East Bristol Auctions, April.

Legoland 6986 Mission Commander. An original vintage (1989) unboxed Legoland set No. 6986 Mission Commander. Vendor assures us the set is complete but this remains unchecked by us. Original instruction manual and x3 minifigures present. Sold for £55, East Bristol Auctions, April.

Legoland 6074 Black Falcons Fortress. An original vintage (1986) boxed Legoland set No. 6074 Black Falcons Fortress. Set appearing complete but remains unchecked by us. Within original box and instructions present. Great set. Sold for £80, East Bristol Auctions, April.

Lego Star Wars 75105 Millennium Falcon an original boxed Lego set No. 75105 Millennium Falcon with x7 minifigures and instructions present. Sold for £75, East Bristol Auctions, April.

Lego System Set 6766 Rapid River Village. An original vintage 1997 set No. 6766 'Rapid River Village'. Unboxed but with instructions present. Sold for £70, East Bristol Auctions, April.

Legoland Set 6067 Guarded Inn. An original vintage (1986) boxed Legoland set No. 6067 Castle Knights Guarded Inn. Set appearing complete but this remains unchecked by us. Within original box and instructions present. Sold for £90, East Bristol Auctions, April.

Lego Creator Expert Set 10024 Red Baron, an original factory sealed boxed Lego set No.10024 Red Baron aircraft. The retired set sealed and unused, some damage to one side of box. Good example. Sold for £170, East Bristol Auctions, April.

A scarce Lego Space factory sealed set No. 6805 Astro Dasher. Fully factory sealed, and unopened. Box in mint condition. Sold for £165, East Bristol Auctions, April.

Lego Star Wars set number 10227 B-Wing Starfighter, within near mint sealed packaging. Ex shop stock. Sold for £280, Vectis, April.

Lego Star Wars set number 10195 Republic Dropship with AT-OT Walker, within near mint sealed packaging. Ex shop stock. Sold for £700, Vectis, April.

Lego Star Wars set number 75055 Imperial Star Destroyer, within excellent to near mint sealed packaging. Ex shop stock. Sold for £220, Vectis, April.

Lego Star Wars set number 8129 AT-AT Walker, within excellent to near mint sealed packaging. Ex shop stock. Sold for £160, Vectis, April.

Lego Star Wars set number 7964 Republic Frigate, within excellent to near mint sealed packaging. Ex shop stock. Sold for £180, Vectis, April.

Lego Star Wars set number 7665 Republic Cruiser, within excellent to near mint sealed packaging. Ex shop stock. Sold for £190, Vectis, April.

Lego Star Wars set number 8096 Emperor Palpatine's Shuttle, within excellent to near mint sealed packaging. Ex shop stock. Sold for £70, Vectis, April.

Lego Star Wars set number 9526 Palpatine's Arrest, within excellent to near mint sealed packaging. Ex shop stock. Sold for £260, Vectis, April.

Lego Star Wars set number 7961 Darth Maul's Sith Infiltrator, within excellent to near mint sealed packaging. Ex shop stock. Sold for £80, Vectis, April.

Lego Star Wars set number 75025 Jedi Defender Class Cruiser, within excellent to near mint sealed packaging. Ex shop stock. Sold for £150, Vectis, April.

Lego Star Wars set number 9500 Sith Fury-Class Interceptor, within excellent to near mint sealed packaging. Ex shop stock. Sold for £150, Vectis, April.

Lego Star Wars set number 7879 Hoth Echo Base, within excellent to near mint sealed packaging. Ex shop stock. Sold for £110, Vectis, April.

Lego Star Wars set number 75054 AT-AT, within excellent to near mint sealed packaging. Ex shop stock. Sold for £120, Vectis, April.

Lego Star Wars set number 7962 Anakin's and Sebulba's Podracers, within excellent to near mint sealed packaging. Ex shop stock. Sold for £100, Vectis, April.

Iron Man #1 (1968 Marvel, UK cover price). Sealed and graded 6.5 by PGX Fine+. Off white to white pages. Origin of Iron Man retold. Gene Colan, Johnny Craig cover & interior art. Flat/unfolded, supplied slabbed and sealed PGX Fine+ Graded 96.5. Sold for £480, Excalibur Auctions, May.

Amazing Spider-Man #47 (1967 Marvel, UK price variant). Kraven the Hunter, Green Goblin appearances. John Romita Sr cover and interior art. Flat/unfolded. Sold for £55, Excalibur Auctions, May.

Amazing Spider-Man #46 (1967 Marvel, UK price variant). Origin and first appearance of the Shocker. John Romita Sr cover and interior art. Flat/unfolded. Sold for £48, Excalibur Auctions, May.

Amazing Spider-Man #55 (1967 Marvel, UK cover price). Doctor Octopus appearance. John Romita Sr cover and interior art. Flat/unfolded. Sold for £32, Excalibur Auctions, May.

Iron Man & Sub-Mariner #1 (1968 Marvel). Iron Man story continued from Tales of Suspense #99 and continues in Iron Man #1. Sub-Mariner story continued from Tales to Astonish #101. Gene Colan, Bill Everett cover with Colan and Johnny Craig interior art. Flat/unfolded. Sold for £140, Excalibur Auctions, May.

Silver Surfer #1 (1968 Marvel). Silver Surfer's origin is retold in more detail. The Watcher backup stories begin with his origin. John Buscema cover with Buscema and Gene Colan interior art. Flat/unfolded. Sold for £750, Excalibur Auctions, May.

Moon Knight #1 (1980 Marvel). Origin of Moon Knight and first appearance of the villain Raoul Bushman. Bill Sienkiewicz cover and interior art. Flat/unfolded. Sold for £75, Excalibur Auctions, May.

Uncanny X-Men annual #4 (1980 Marvel). Doctor Strange appearance. John Romita Jr cover and interior art. Flat/unfolded. Sold for £18, Excalibur Auctions, May.

Uncanny X-Men #99 (1976 Marvel, UK price variant). First appearance of Black Tom Cassidy and Sentinels appearance. Dave Cockrum cover and interior art. Flat/unfolded. Sold for £22, Excalibur Auctions, May.

Uncanny X-Men #100 (1976 Marvel, UK price variant). The original X-Men vs the new X-Men, and origin of Phoenix. Dave Cockrum cover and interior art. Flat/unfolded. Sold for £32, Excalibur Auctions, May.

Uncanny X-Men #108 (1977 Marvel, UK price variant). Starjammers appearance and Corsair revealed to be the father of Cyclops and Havok. Dave Cockrum, John Byrne cover and interior art, John Byrne's first issue as artist. Sold for £15, Excalibur Auctions, May.

Uncanny X-Men #109 (1978 Marvel UK price variant). First appearance of Vindicator (aka Guardian, called Weapon Alpha in this issue). Dave Cockrum cover with John Byrne interior art. Flat/unfolded. Sold for £28, Excalibur Auctions, May.

Uncanny X-Men #129 (1980 Marvel, UK price variant). First appearances of Kitty Pryde, Emma Frost, Sebastian Shaw, and the Hellfire Club. John Byrne and Terry Austin cover and interior art. Flat/unfolded. Sold for £110, Excalibur Auctions, May.

Royal Doulton The Rupert Bear Collection Out for the Day figurine, RB 14, 2005, near mint to mint, with certificate and box. Sold for £30, Vectis, June.

Royal Doulton The Rupert Bear Collection Rupert's Silver Trumpet, RB 8, 2003, near mint to mint, with certificate and box. Sold for £45, Vectis, June.

Royal Doulton The Rupert Bear Collection Rupert, Bill and the Mysterious Car figurine, RB 11, LE 2,500, 2003, from Rupert and The Travel Machine, near mint to mint, with certificate and box. Sold for £40, Vectis, June.

Royal Doulton The Rupert Bear Collection Tempted to Trespass figurine, RB 5, LE 2,500, 2003, Rupert and the Travel Machine-Rupert and Bill Badger are out for a walk in the snow, near mint to mint, with certificate and box. Sold for £35, Vectis, June.

Royal Doulton Rupert the Bear Collection Rupert Takes a Ski-ing Lesson figurine, RB 20, 2003, from Rupert and the Arrow, near mint to mint, with certificate and box. Sold for £30, Vectis, June.

Royal Doulton The Rupert Bear Collection Rupert Rides Home figurine, RB 4, LE 2,500, 2003, from Rupert and the Jumping Fish, near mint to mint, with certificate and box. Sold for £25, Vectis, June.

Royal Doulton The Rupert Bear Collection Rupert and the King figurine, RB 21, LE 2,000, 2005, to celebrate the 85th Birthday of Rupert the Bear, some crazing to glaze on underside of base, otherwise near mint to mint, with certificate and box. Sold for £35, Vectis, June.

Royal Doulton The Rupert Bear Collection Going Out Late figurine, RB 18, 2005, near mint to mint, with certificate and box. Sold for £60, Vectis, June.

Royal Doulton The Rupert Bear Collection We Meant to Put Them Back figurine, RB 16, 2005, near mint to mint, with certificate and box. Sold for £40, Vectis, June.

Royal Doulton The Rupert Bear Collection Edward Trunk Pretending to be an Outlaw figurine, RB 2, 2003, near mint to mint, with certificate and box. Sold for £15, Vectis, June.

Royal Doulton The Rupert Bear Collection Rupert's Toy Railway figurine, RB 1, LE 2,500, 2003, Rupert's Toy Railway Puzzle first appeared in the 1950 Rupert Annual, near mint to mint, with certificate and box. Sold for £30, Vectis, June.

Royal Doulton The Rupert Bear Collection Banging On His Drum figurine, RB 17, 2005, near mint to mint, with certificate and box. Sold for £15, Vectis, June.

Royal Doulton The Rupert Bear Collection Algy Pug - Looking Like Robin Hood figurine, RB 6, 2003, near mint to mint, with certificate and box. Sold for £15, Vectis, June.

Royal Doulton The Rupert Bear Collection The Imp of Spring figurine, RB 15, LE 2,500, 2005, some red paint has flaked away from imp's left leg where it's attached to base, otherwise near mint, with certificate and box. Sold for £35, Vectis, June.

Royal Doulton The Rupert Bear Collection Podgy Lands With A Bump figurine, RB 9, 2003, near mint to mint, with certificate and box. Sold for £15, Vectis, June.

Lego Legoland 6285 Black Seas Barracuda, an original vintage (1989) boxed Black Seas Barracuda / Pirate Ship. The set believed complete but remains unchecked. Sold for £220, East Bristol Auctions, July.

Lego The Hobbit An Unexpected Journey 79002 Attack Of The Wargs, an original boxed set. The now retired set appearing to be resealed to one side but the vendor confirmed that the set is 100% complete with instructions present. From a large private collection of Lego. Sold for £45, East Bristol Auctions, July.

Lego City 60093 Deep Sea Helicopter, an original boxed Lego set. The now retired set appearing to be resealed to one side but the vendor confirmed that the set in 100% complete with instructions present. Sold for £28, East Bristol Auctions, July.

Lego Star Wars Set 75149 Resistance X-Wing Fighter, an original boxed Lego set. The now retired set appearing to be resealed to one side but the vendor confirmed that the set is 100% complete with instructions present. Sold for £40, East Bristol Auctions, July.

Lego Star Wars Set 75102 Poe's X-Wing Fighter, an original boxed Lego Star Wars set. The now retired set appearing to possibly be resealed to one side but the vendor confirmed that the set is 100% complete with instructions present. Sold for £45, East Bristol Auctions, July.

Lego DC Universe Super Heroes 6860 The Batcave, an original boxed Lego set. The now retired set appearing to be resealed to one side but the vendor confirmed that the set is 100% complete with instructions present. Sold for £35, East Bristol Auctions, July.

Lego Harry Potter Set 4708 Hogwarts Express, an original boxed Lego set. The now retired set appearing factory sealed within original box. From a large private collection of Lego. Sold for £150, East Bristol Auctions, July.

Lego Creator Set 4997 Transport Ferry, an original boxed Lego 3 in 1 set. The now retired set appearing to be resealed but the vendor confirmed the set is 100% complete with instructions present. Sold for £40, East Bristol Auctions, July.

Lego Creator Set 10266 Nasa Apollo 11 Lunar Lander, an original factory sealed boxed Lego set. Great set. Sold for £65, East Bristol Auctions, July.

Lego Star Wars Set 9493 X-Wing Star Fighter, an original Lego Star Wars set. Now retired set, appearing to be resealed, complete with instructions present. Sold for £45, East Bristol Auctions, July.

Lego Creator Set 10265 Ford Mustang, an original factory sealed boxed Lego set. Great set. From a large private collection of Lego. Sold for £75, East Bristol Auctions, July.

Lego City Set 7897 Passenger Train, an original boxed Lego City set. Retired set, appearing to be resealed to one side, complete with instructions present. Sold for £65, East Bristol Auctions, July.

Lego Set 80103 Dragon Boat Race, an original factory sealed boxed Lego set. Great set. From a large private collection of Lego. Sold for £40, East Bristol Auctions, July.

Lego Ninjago Masters of Spinjitzu 70732 City of Stiix, an original boxed set appearing to be resealed but the vendor assures us the set is 100% complete with instructions present. Sold for £80, East Bristol Auctions, July.

Lego Star Wars Set 6211 Imperial Star Destroyer, an original boxed set. The now retired set appearing to be resealed but the vendor assures us the set is 100% complete with instructions present. Sold for £100, East Bristol Auctions, July.

A classic USA reproduction pressed steel child's pedal car, American, circa 2000, the silver red and black vintage style car with red upholstered seats, chrome plated parts, wooden steering wheel, balloon wheels with solid rubber tyres. Sold for £80, C&T Auctioneers, September.

Tri-ang 'The Duke Express' child's pedal train, English, circa 1960, red painted pressed steel body with black grill and steering wheel, black rubber chimney and chrome bell, 'Duke Express' sticker to front, white solid wheels with solid rubber tyres. In good, restored condition. Sold for £150, C&T Auctioneers, September.

A scarce M & G (Morellett & Guerineae) Honda child's motor racing pedal car, French circa 1970, red painted pressed steel body with brown painted bucket seat, cast aluminium steering wheel with V8 logo, rear painted roll bar and dummy engine, silver spoked wheels with solid rubber tyres, R.N.8, Honda and checker band decors. In excellent restored condition. Sold for £520, C&T Auctioneers, September.

A scarce Pines Chitty-Chitty Bang-Bang moulded plastic child's pedal car, Italian 1970s, finished in gold with black plastic mud guards and running boards, red plastic upholstered seat and steering wheel, Chitty-Chitty Bang-Bang décor to bonnet, rear metal bumper, front metal grill with lights, GEN.11 number plate, red spoked wheels with solid rubber tyres, plastic silver and bronze side exhaust pipes and pull-out red and yellow side wings. In good condition. Sold for £480, C&T Auctioneers, September.

Lines Brothers wooden Double Decker General bus, with electric interior light, 1920s, painted in red and cream with grey roof, interior seating and stairs, tinplate grill and steering wheel to open drivers cab, gold painted General to sides, service 123 plaque, paper Liverpool Street destinations, pressed steel wheel hubs with rubber tyres. Sold for £280, C&T Auctioneers, September.

Scarce Tri-ang pressed steel and wooden Evening News delivery van, 1930s, painted in orange and black, pressed steel cab and solid wheels, wooden back with rear opening doors and tin Evening News tinplate plaque to sides and EX 8025 number plate, replaced front grill. Sold for £440, C&T Auctioneers, September.

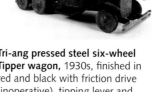

Tri-ang pressed steel six-wheel Tipper wagon, 1930s, finished in red and black with friction drive (inoperative), tipping lever and Tri-ang Transport decals to sides, lacks tailgate. Sold for £170, C&T Auctioneers, September.

Scarce Tri-ang Noah's Ark complete with animals, circa 1955, red and cream plywood construction, L.28" (71 cm), H.15" (40 cm), with fourteen plastic animals with wheels, 2x boar, 2x camels, 2x Hippo, 2x Rhino, 2x lions, 2x tigers, 2x elephants, rubber Noah & Mrs Noah and wooden ramp, in excellent original condition. Sold for £190, C&T Auctioneers, September.

Fantastic Four No.81 / #81 December 1968, CGC 9.0 VF/near mint graded and slabbed. Sold for £100, Sheffield Auction Galleries, September.

A Palitoy ' Peter Brough's Archie Andrews Ventriloquist Doll', appears to have been used very little, with paper instructions. Sold for £50, Sheffield Auction Galleries, September.

A boxed Moko "Muffin" Junior Puppet, strings repaired, box poor. Sold for £35, Sheffield Auction Galleries, September.

A boxed Hasbro GI Joe 'Timeless Collection 40th Anniversary Set 'Footlocker and 1964 Action Soldier'. The set appears mint presented in a very good overall box with some crushing to one corner and general storage imperfections. Sold for £45, British Toy Auctions, September.

A boxed Action Man '40th Anniversary' Combat Action Soldier Set from Modellers Loft. The set appears mint within an excellent presentation box with some minor storage wear. Sold for £45, British Toy Auctions, September.

A limited edition 50th Anniversary Cooper Climax F-1 (1959) by Scalextric, No. 0774, vehicle appears mint in excellent box. Sold for £45, British Toy Auctions, September.

ebuys

We round up some of the best collecting highlights sold throughout the year on eBay.

No matter which way you look at it, eBay revolutionised the collecting market - some would say for the best, while others may think it's actually been for the worst. However, there's certainly no disputing that eBay does throw up some fantastic collectables that you might not find anywhere else.

Back when it was launched in 1995 it must have seemed like a curious website that might occasionally have some interesting items for sale but since then it has grown into one of the biggest websites in the world with a turnover of millions. Of course, back in those early days you could use the website to pick up a bargain because not many people used it and sellers weren't always aware of an item's value. However, now there are millions of collectors around the world who ensure the price on eBay is often pushed up well above what the same toy may have sold for at a traditional auction or toy fair - as you will probably see from the items listed here.

eBay can also be a useful tool when you're checking to see how much your toys might be worth, as you can quickly search for similar pieces listed on the website. However, don't fall into the trap of looking at a 'Buy it Now' price for a current listing and thinking your toy is worth the same. The best thing to do is tick the 'sold listings' box when searching so you'll get a clearer picture of what items sold and how much they actually sold for. Although even then, make sure the item in question wasn't re-listed at a later date if the original sale fell through. ■

⬆An original Palitoy Star Wars Return of the Jedi Boba Fett figure. He was sold in mint condition, on his card and had been AFA Graded 85. **Sold for £1800 (36 bids).**

⬆A tinplate Scalextric Austin Healey in blue/ cream. Overall a pretty car, with original paint, original driver and a strong working motor. Would benefit from some care and attention. **Sold for £480 (21 bids).**

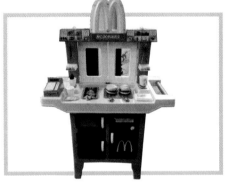

⬆A McDonalds Drive Thru toy kitchen, with working sound effects and play food (burgers, nuggets and fries). All items were original and the instructions were included too. **Sold for £232 (32 bids).**

⬆This 1993 Hasbro My Little Pony figure had been found in the stock room of an old toy shop. Obviously forgotten about this Baby Candy was in excellent condition, with a mint carded back. **Sold for £785 (21 bids).**

⬆A Tri-ang Spot-On No.117 Jones Crane, in excellent condition for its age. This rare version also came with a collector's card. **Sold for £570 (3 bids).**

⬆This LEGO Galaxy Explorer Set 928, from 1979, was in its original box and complete with all parts and instruction leaflets - it had never been opened or played with! **Sold for £1852 (20 bids).**

✦**A LEGO Green Grocer Building Set 10185 dating from 2008.** The owner had never got around to building it so all the pieces were still bagged. **Sold for £1020 (8 bids).**

✦**A Matchbox Lesney No.74 Mobile Canteen,** sold in excellent condition and with the original box. Sadly, some of the decal was missing. **Sold for £909 (26 bids).**

✦**We don't often see tractors in these pages** but this Universal Hobbies Case IH Maxxum MX150 in 1/32 scale is a great example. There were some light marks to the box, but otherwise in great condition. **Sold for £1500 (18 bids).**

✦**A mint condition Matchbox Lesney Superfast No.32 Leyland Tanker,** in a rare red and white NAMC livery. It was the nicest one the seller had ever seen… **Sold for £870 (28 bids).**

✦**Thundercats! Hooo… A Lion-o action figure from the TV series,** in mint condition on its original card. He was UK graded AFA 80 overall. **Sold for £850 (18 bids).**

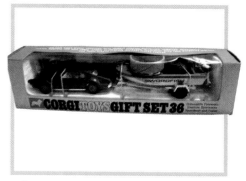

✦**This Corgi Toys Gift Set 36, Oldsmobile Toronado, speed boat and trailer** dates from the late 1960s. The model had the odd scuff mark, as did the original box. **Sold for £474 (33 bids).**

✦**Originally purchased in 1984 for £1.59, this Star Wars Yak Face figure** was part of the 'Last 17'. He had been in a display case all his life so was still in mint condition. **Sold for £1375 (9 bids).**

✦**A Dinky Toys No.903 Foden Flat Truck,** in a rare red and yellow colour variation. Dating from 1954 it was in near mint condition with only a small chip to the paint. **Sold for £535 (25 bids).**

✦**This 1/18 CMC model of a 1961 Ferrari 250 GT Berlinetta SWB** was in very good condition. It was sold in the original packaging, but had no certificate or paperwork with it. **Sold for £520 (17 bids).**

✦**Old MacDonald had a farm… or rather a Corgi Toys Agriculture Gift Set No.5!** The seller had owned this set since childhood and it was in excellent, complete condition. **Sold for £491 (18 bids).**

✦**A rare plastic Britains Super Deetail Kneeling Paratrooper.** The figure was in a very good, although used, condition. **Sold for £271 (27 bids).**

✦**A rare Hornby Meccano vintage tinplate duck toy,** complete with its original key and box. A very different speed boat to add to your collection. **Sold for £910 (30 bids).**

↟Made in Spain this Scalextric Ferrari GT330, in blue, was in full working order. It was in used condition with some brown spotting to the top of the car but no splits or cracks. **Sold for £5100 (10 bids).**

↟A rare Lili Ledy Star Wars Removable Hood Jawa, graded UKG 85 Graded and with its authenticity certificate. A great buy for the lucky winner! **Sold for £1209 (35 bids).**

↟A vintage Scalextric C70 Bugatti Type 59, in beautiful green. Overall the body work was in good condition, however, the top half of the aero windscreen had broken off. **Sold for £408 (15 bids).**

↟A Masters of the Universe vintage He-Man figure, graded UKG 85% and sold within a protective Perspex case. He caused a bit of a stir and drew plenty of bids! **Sold for £4000 (34 bids).**

↟A late variant of the Matchbox Lesney No.73 RAF Pressure Refueller with 10x24 tread black plastic wheels, much less common than the grey wheeled version. The paintwork is generally excellent. **Sold for £2500 (52 bids).**

↟A Corgi Toys No.310 Chevrolet Corvette Stingray, with a rare metallic copper finish. The headlights were still intact and the suspension was firm – an excellent auction find! **Sold for £465 (29 bids).**

↟A Kenner MASK Split Seconds Skybolt jet fighter and thruster car, sold here with an American version box. It came graded 80 and the box showed minimal age wear. **Sold for £1270 (10 bids).**

↟A mint condition Matchbox 26B Cement Lorry. This lovely example from the 1950s came with its original box. **Sold for £1227 (2 bids).**

↟This classic LEGO Kings Castle (No.6080) had lived in the seller's loft since it was first bought in 1984. As such it was in still in mint condition and had never been opened. **Sold for £1220 (27 bids).**

↟Made by Moko, the German toy maker, this clockwork soldier was still in reasonable condition for its age. It was missing the key but the wind-up mechanism still moved, striking the drum. **Sold for £726 (39 bids).**

↟Released for the 2016 San Diego Comic Con this LEGO Marvel BrickHeadz set contained Marvel characters Black Panther and Doctor Strange. It was sold here in mint condition. **Sold for £710 (22 bids).**

↟This 1987 Thundercats Tongue-A-Saurus was advertised as extremely rare by the seller. In used condition, the action lever still worked to make the mouth open and tongue lash out. **Sold for £2850 (19 bids).**